Authentic Assessment

Authentic Assessment
A Guide for Elementary Teachers

Kathleen Montgomery

University of Scranton

New York   San Francisco   Boston
London   Toronto   Sydney   Tokyo   Singapore   Madrid
Mexico City   Munich   Paris   Cape Town   Hong Kong   Montreal

Publisher: Priscilla McGeehon
Acquisition Editor: Amy Cronin
Development Manager: Lisa Pinto
Marketing Manager: Marilyn Borysek
Production Manager: Mark Naccarelli
Project Coordination, Text Design, and Electronic Page Makeup: WestWords, Inc.
Cover Design/Manager: Nancy Danahy
Cover Designer: Keithley and Associates
Cover Photo: © PhotoDisc
Printer Buyer: Roy Pickering
Printer and Binder: The Maple-Vail Book Manufacturing Group
Cover Printer: The Lehigh Press, Inc.

Library of Congress Cataloging-in-Publication Data

Montgomery, Kathleen
    Authentic assessment : a guide for elementary teachers / Kathleen Montgomery.
        p. cm.
    Includes bibliographical references (p. 115) and index.
    ISBN 0-321-03782-0
        1. Educational tests and measurements—United States. 2. Education,
    Elementary—United States. I. Title.

    LB3051 .M775 2000
    372.17—dc21
                                                                00-025840

Copyright © 2001 by Addison Wesley Longman, Inc.

Please visit our website at http://www.awl.com

ISBN 0-321-03782-0

12345678910—MA—03 02 01 00

For Jessica
You are never given a wish without also
being given the power to make it true.

Contents

PART II
Designing and Using Rubrics for Assessment

PART III
Portfolios and Assessment

PART **IV**

Using Assessments for Grading and Reporting

Introduction

This book is for preservice and in-service elementary teachers who believe that students should become self-regulated, lifelong learners and who suspect that the research on the "new assessments" is the means toward that end. It is for teachers whose precious time need not be taken by wandering through the maze of terms and definitions in the assessment literature in order to glean a few good practices. Finally, this book is for teachers who perceive that what students have done successfully is proof of what they have learned. *Authentic Assessment: A Practical Guide for Elementary Teachers* is a union of research and practice that passed the stringent tests of hundreds of excellent elementary teachers in several school districts in upstate New York. I am very grateful to these teachers for their willingness to wrestle with new ideas to make them even better.

Initially, these teachers revealed that they did not know the difference between authentic assessment and performance assessment. Many commented that both kinds of assessment sounded too time consuming and some admitted that they did not see the benefits in changing past procedures. Although some writers make a distinction between authentic assessment and performance assessment, others (e.g., Reed, 1993; Wiggins, 1989) treat the terms as equivalent, as this book does. This view eliminated extraneous barriers for everyone and enabled teachers to closely examine the research on the need to change assessment methods.

The teachers agreed that, from today's cognitive perspective, meaningful learning is reflective, constructive, and self-regulated. Students were seen as creators of their own unique knowledge structures and teachers shared wonderful ideas and activities that exemplified learning by doing as well as methods to assist students in self-reflection. It wasn't long before the teachers agreed that *exclusive* use of conventional methods of assessment was inadequate for assessing all the learning that took place in their classrooms. This is not to suggest that conventional assessments no longer have a place in education, but that such assessments need not dominate classroom assessment as they have for the past half-century.

Additionally, teachers recognized that designing and implementing authentic assessment methods would be time-consuming and wondered what kind of administrative and district support would be forthcoming. These concerns were well founded and all are well documented in the literature. For example, reported constraints to authentic assessment include the following:

- Authentic assessment strategies are often costly in terms of both time and money (Bracey, 1993);
- Students often lack experience and skill in responding to open-ended, interpretive, applied, and higher-order essay questions (Liftig, Liftig, & Eaker, 1992);
- The linguistic demands of many authentic assessment approaches may result in some equity issues (Rudner, 1993); and
- The increased validity of authentic assessment is often associated with a decrease in reliability (Rudner, 1993; Worthen, 1993; & Bowers, 1989).

While these concerns are real, they are certainly not insurmountable. Researchers, teachers, administrators, school boards, and others must continue to give time, money, and energy into making sure that authentic assessments are implemented in the best possible way so that effective school reform can become a reality for all our children.

As teachers worked through concerns about and benefits of authentic assessment, it became apparent to everyone that the use of authentic assessment would validate and enhance much of what teachers were already doing. Those teachers who had inclusionary classrooms were especially grateful as we created observation instruments, rubrics, checklist, and self-assessment forms, all of which would aid teachers in gathering data for students with special needs. It wasn't long, however, until everyone recognized that good instructional practices and corresponding methods of assessment served all learners equally well.

As we worked, teachers spontaneously recalled personal stories where they felt their own learning could have been strengthened through the use of authentic assessment. The following story illustrates the power of planning authentic tasks and assessments: Donna Wertheimer, a friend and colleague of mine, listened to me talk about the capabilities of using methods of authentic assessment. All of a sudden she excitedly related what had happened to her in her undergraduate program. She was asked to write a children's book by her "kiddy-lit" instructor, a task she thought would be easy. But there was no rubric, no checklist, no form of authentic assessment with specific evaluation criteria to guide her through the process of writing a book. As a result, many of her classmates floundered through the task, but Donna spent hours in the library trying to figure out the critical attributes of a children's book. She made her own checklist and rubric for success. As a result of her work, she:

- read over one hundred children's books;
- examined the work of numerous illustrators;
- checked out the criteria for the Caldecott and Newbury Awards;
- taught herself how to use readability scales;
- researched the topics and interests appropriate for children at a variety of levels; **and**

wrote a book of which she was very proud. She received an "A" from her instructor, but so did several students with mediocre children's books. After marriage and the birth of a son, Donna wrote two more children's books for her son on topics for which she could not find existing books. Donna is now a highly competent college librarian, surrounded by books. With the use of authentic assessment, the children's literature instructor could have been more discriminating with assigning grades and, more importantly, perhaps a few more potential authors would have been discovered.

Learning and assessment become one and the same with authentic assessment. The use of authentic assessment is engaging, motivating, and stimulating to students and teachers alike. Start small, perhaps with a favorite project or a single unit. Involve the students in the task of setting up assessments. Give some power away to students. It's only perceived power and everyone will benefit.

CHAPTER 1

Making the Case for Authentic Assessment

Maria Ruiz was completing her second set of report cards for her third graders. As a first-year teacher, she was proud of her ability to get the most from her students. She smiled when she thought of reading Justin's journal when he wrote, "You are a good teacher Ms. Ruiz cause you are always fair and you are nice besides." Fair and nice. Quite a compliment, but right now she didn't feel fair or nice. There seemed to be no place on the report card for the wonderful projects and presentations students had completed—all the fun things that were impossible to grade using the present system that required a letter grade for isolated subjects. "Maybe I need to change my instruction, " she thought, "and give more objective tests."

The dilemma facing Ms. Ruiz is the same for good elementary teachers everywhere when asked to quantify learning for reporting purposes by giving letter or percentage grades to separate content areas. These teachers, who plan integrated, complex, and engaging learning experiences for their students, find it very difficult to equate such instruction with grades on conventional report cards. In fact, the whole area of assessment today is issue laden and problematic. Conventional assessment practices consist primarily of pencil-and-paper activities that measure single attribute tasks with a near exclusive emphasis on individual assessment. They do not seem to address such issues as the processes of acquisition of knowledge, the ability to communicate information, or the ability to solve problems. There is much confusion about the relationship between process and product and how these are reflected in a grade. Often, the relationships between pedagogical goals and the grades on tests or projects are not made clear to students (Placier, 1995).

Further compounding the discussion of assessment practices is the choice of terms used. For example, "traditional" assessments connote "old-fashioned" to some while the use of the term "authentic" assessments makes one wonder if other kinds of assessment are "bogus". The same is true of "alternative" assessment that implies a kind of second-class choice compared to "conventional" methods that infer that other assessment methods are "unconventional". Unhappily, this book offers no solution to this dilemma of connotations except to say that exclusive use of *any* single method of assessment is highly undesirable. Instead, practitioners should understand the meaning behind the assessment term and appropriately match assessments with instruction and curriculum. School districts should invest in making sure that in-service teachers have every opportunity to learn about the rationale behind assessment methods and how to use them. The purposes of assessment, such as the following by Airasian (1994), should be an ongoing topic for staff development activities:

- diagnosing student problems
- making judgments about student academic performance
- determining student placement
- planning and conducting instruction
- providing feedback and incentives to students
- establishing and maintaining the social equilibrium of the classroom

School districts must provide the time and money necessary for teachers to understand the purposes of instruction and which assessment methods will help realize those purposes.

There has been a renewed interest in examining assessment practices, as evidenced by an increase in professional literature (Riley, et al. 1994). Numerous articles are devoted to such topics as the relationships between and among the areas of curriculum, instruction, and assessment; the understanding and examination of relationships between conventional assessment practices and their worth in measuring learning; the effects of grading on teaching and learning (Eison, Janzow, & Pollio, 1993); reporting performance with a single letter grade; and the purposes for placing grades on student writing and project work (Ekstrom & Villegas, 1994; Goulden and Griffin, 1995). In many of these articles, the impression is given that there is no longer any place for conventional, or traditional, methods of assessment in education. In fact, the question common to many authors examining assessment reform is *when* should conventional assessments be used, not *if* they should be used.

Since this book addresses assessment practices at the classroom level, the decision when to use conventional assessment will be an individual one made teacher by teacher. Many teachers would probably say that conventional assessment would be most helpful when the need arose to measure the attainment of content knowledge. For example, teachers who plan interdisciplinary instruction attribute equal importance to content and process

(Wood, 1997) because they expect their students to amass facts and develop concepts while they practice important academic learning processes that will become the models for later exploratory behaviors. In addition to using authentic assessment methods, these teachers would likely select conventional forms of assessment such as matching, multiple choice, or fill-in-the-blank tests in order to measure the content acquisition of students. Conventional assessments are certainly a piece of the total assessment pie, but they no longer represent the entire pie.

For example, authentic assessment offers new ways of looking at assessment and evaluation. First, the emphasis on aligning assessment with curriculum and instruction helps teachers examine whether they really are testing what they teach (Darling-Hammond, Ancess, & Falk, 1995). Second, holistic approaches to assessment offer teachers possibilities for considering process and progress as well as product (Belanoff & Dickson, 1991). Third, student self-assessment tools give students ownership along with responsibility for learning (Dart & Clarke, 1991; Fazey, 1993). Fourth, the use of rubrics with detailed criteria, which are explained in advance, provide students with clear guidelines for preparing work (Williams, 1992). Finally, authentic assessment methods are linked not only to curriculum and instruction in school settings but also to application in the real world.

THE TERMINOLOGY SURROUNDING ASSESSMENT

In the literature and in practice, new terminology has been coined or old words have been used in new ways. Once teachers are operating from a common language, much of the mystery and trepidation concerning the "right" ways to make and use assessments will disappear. For example, some authors have attempted to differentiate between student assessment and evaluation by saying that assessment is based on a decision about whether the student has achieved the criteria for the objective while evaluation carries an implication of a judgment reached after assessing multiple forms of data (Eby, 1997). The two terms, however, are used interchangeably throughout the literature and in the schools. Most teachers agree that evaluation is used synonymous with grading and that one piece of work can be evaluated at the same time it is being assessed. This book will use the terms interchangeably. Given below is a list of terms and working definitions that this book will use to discuss the issues of the new, or authentic, assessments.

> *Assessment and Evaluation:* This is the process of collecting data about a student from one or more sources, comparing the data to criteria or standards previously set, and making a decision or judgment based on this information.

Authentic Task: This is a real-life activity, performance, or challenge that mirrors those faced by experts in the particular field; it is complex and multidimensional and requires higher levels of cognitive thinking such as problem solving and critical thinking.

Authentic Assessment: According to Wiggins (1989), authentic assessment should involve an authentic task and students should be asked to demonstrate their control over the essential knowledge being taught by using the information in a way that reveals their level of understanding. The evaluation criteria should be understood by the students from the start so that they can self-assess their work by applying the criteria.

Critical Thinking: Thinking that uses higher-order mental processes, such as analyzing arguments carefully, seeing alternative points of view, evaluating alternatives, and reaching sound conclusions.

Higher-order Thinking Skills: Thinking skills that require relatively complex cognitive operations such as concept formation, analysis, and problem solving that commonly employ one or more skills.

Holistic Grading: This is the practice of giving an overall evaluation to a product without analyzing the strengths or weaknesses of each part of the product separately. In a writing assignment, for instance, grammar, punctuation, and spelling would not be graded individually but would be considered in the overall sense of fluency and expression of ideas.

Measurement: Measurement involves collecting data or information from the environment through the use of the senses. Examples of formal measurements are tests and quizzes. Examples of informal measurements are anecdotal records of a student's behavior or notes from a student interview. One form of measurement used in authentic assessment is a rubric.

Metacognition: Metacognitions are the self-appraisal and self-regulation processes used in learning, thinking, reasoning, and problem solving.

Portfolio: A portfolio is a collection of student work showing student reflection and progress or achievement over time in one or more areas.

Portfolio Assessment: This includes a selective collection of student work and self-assessment that is used to show progress over time with regard to specific criteria.

Rubric: A rubric is an assessment device that uses clearly specified evaluation criteria and proficiency levels that measure student achievement of those criteria. The criteria provide descriptions of each level of performance in terms of what students are able to do. The criteria for a task are known in advance by the students. Products, process, and/or product may all be evaluated by means of rubrics.

Self-assessment: Self-assessment is an appraisal by a student of his or her own work or learning processes.

Conventional Assessment: Methods of conventional, or traditional, assessment are usually limited to paper and pencil, one-answer questions that rarely ask students to explain their reasoning.

INFLUENCE OF SCHOOL REFORM

In the 1970's the United States experienced a demand for accountability in educational endeavors. State legislators, departments of education, and school districts wanted a way to know that students were learning in our nation's schools. Standardized tests were the accountability test of choice of schools around the nation primarily because they were easy to score and familiar to educators. School districts began publishing the test scores to their communities, which caused competition among teachers of the same subject and between schools as well. As a result, schools were pressured by the community to get better and better scores and they began teaching to the test creating "skill and drill" instruction (Popham, 1993).

As schools continued to teach to the tests, the scores have become poor assessments of students' overall abilities. Several researchers have found that classwork that is oriented toward recognizing the answers to multiple-choice questions does not heighten students' proficiency in areas that are not tested such as analysis, complex problem solving, and written and oral expression (Koretz, 1983; Haney & Madaus, 1986; Darling-Hammond & Wise, 1985). It appears clear that if classroom instructional time is spent on rote learning, then the critical thinking behaviors of students will suffer. Linda Darling-Hammond (1994) says that, since about 1970 when standardized tests began to be used for a wider variety of accountability purposes, basic skills test scores have been increasing slightly while assessments of higher-order thinking skills have declined in virtually all subject areas.

At the same time, throughout the last decade, newspapers have reported that American students score low among the nations of the world on standardized tests in almost every subject. Apparently, a large percentage of American students cannot match world capitals with the corresponding country nor can these students name the current members of the United States Supreme Court. Given this news, the following question comes to mind: "Is it our purpose to give students the most number of facts they can memorize, or is it our purpose to teach students where to find the answers to their questions as the need arises?" In the age of such massive amounts of information, it seems obvious that time would be better spent in information search strategies.

School reform efforts agree that this is indeed a time when American schools are being challenged to provide opportunities to achieve at much higher levels. This does not mean, however, greater opportunities for rote learning. Rather, many states have begun to identify higher standards for learning and set content and performance standards that cannot be measured by low-level tests. The Center for Research on Evaluation, Standards, and Student Testing (CRESST) found that as of 1990, nearly half of all states in the United States were considering implementation of some form of performance or authentic assessment in state-level testing. This includes portfolio assessment, an example of authentic assessment that includes a selective collection of student work and self-assessment. Authentic assessments require students to use acquired knowledge in tasks such as conducting research, writing and discussing a variety of written tasks, or debating important issues. Such assessments have been adopted by many states for statewide assessment purposes.

A common lament from states opting for large-scale authentic assessments is that such assessments are costly and time consuming and stakeholders are resistant to change. These concerns are not insurmountable, according to the Council of Chief State School Officers (Bond, Roeber, & Connealy, 1998) who released the following information on the trends in state student assessment programs:

> In spite of the difficulties states have experienced in implementing non-conventional assessment programs, it is clear that strictly traditional programs are becoming uncommon. States are embracing new forms of assessment and looking for ways to make them work. It is an exciting time in large-scale assessment and as long as the public is brought along, the technical quality issues are resolved, and the cost and time management issues are addressed, a blended assessment program will continue to be the preferred model of state assessment. Going back to the days of "one type fits all" assessment is highly unlikely. (p. 21)

Assessment is at the center of school reform because most researchers and educators reason that methods of assessment will greatly influence instruction and drive school reform into the area of effective teaching practices. Recognizing that the classroom teacher is most acutely aware of the learning context, Farr (1991) cautions that:

> The classroom teacher is in a unique position to see that assessment appropriately matches the learning environment and that measurement is well integrated with instruction. Therefore, there is likely to be increased demand for teachers to construct tests which accurately reflect course content and goals, which are designed to mea-

sure not only facts and procedures but the relationships between them, and which incorporates the broader notion of learning that includes thinking. (p. 294)

In order to assist the classroom teacher toward making these changes in assessment practices, school districts need to provide teachers with appropriate in-service education as well as time to plan for and construct assessments that match constructivist strategies used in today's classrooms.

A move toward more authentic tasks and outcomes thus improves teaching and learning, students have greater clarity about their obligations, and teachers can come to believe that assessment results are both meaningful and useful for improving instruction (Wiggins, 1990). The instructional emphasis should be on student success and on curriculum that meets the needs of every student.

MOVING TOWARD AUTHENTIC ASSESSMENT METHODS

The methods of assessment selected for use are, in large part, determined by educators' beliefs about how people learn. These beliefs are greatly influenced by the prevailing research on learning theory. Early in the twentieth century, E. L. Thorndike (1913) set a quantitative path for the development of tests and measurement. The view at that time was that learning could be broken down into bits of discrete, prerequisite knowledge that could be efficiently measured and reported. Further, it was believed that memorization of basic knowledge could then be used by the student to build complex understanding or conceptual learning without further instructional influence by the teacher.

Today's learning theory research suggests that all learning requires that the learner think and actively construct conceptual learning (Flavell, 1985). Dewey (1916) was a proponent of active learning when he wrote that knowledge and ideas emerged only from a situation (occurring in a social context) in which learners had to draw ideas out of experiences that had meaning and importance to them. Piaget (1973) demonstrated that understanding is built up step by step through active involvement where children must discover relationships and ideas in classroom situations that interest them. Bruner (1966) agrees that learning is an active process in which learners construct new ideas or concepts based upon their current and past knowledge. These constructivist views of learning are summed up best by Brooks and Brooks (1993) who describe instruction in a constructivist classroom as follows:

- *Student autonomy and initiative are accepted and encouraged.* Students who frame questions and issues and then go about analyzing and answering them take responsibility for their own learning and become better problem solvers.

- *The teacher asks open-ended questions and allows adequate wait time for responses.* Reflective thought takes time and is often built on others' ideas and comments.
- *Higher-level thinking is encouraged.* The constructivist teacher challenges students to reach beyond the simple factual response. Students are encouraged to connect and summarize concepts by analyzing, predicting, justifying, and defending their ideas.
- *Students are engaged in dialogue with the teacher and with each other.* Social discourse helps students change or reinforce their ideas.
- *Students are engaged in experiences that challenge hypotheses and encourage discussion.* The constructivist teacher provides ample opportunities for students to test their hypotheses, especially through group discussion of concrete experiences.
- *The class uses raw data, primary sources, manipulatives, physical and interactive materials.* The constructivist approach involves students in real-world possibilities, then helps them generate the abstractions that bind phenomena together.

Effective teaching research, much of which is based on the tenets of constructivism, adds that the teacher's primary responsibility is to plan and implement instruction that will involve the learner in higher-level thinking. Because constructing a correct response differs substantially from recognizing one in a list of potential responses, authentic assessments, including portfolios, are attracting considerable attention (Hakel, 1998). Cognitive learning theory and its constructivist approach to knowledge acquisition support the need to use assessment methods that move away from passive responses by students to active construction of meaning. According to Grabe and Grabe (1998), constructivist learning experiences and appropriate classroom practices include reflective thinking and productivity along with authentic activities, student collaboration, and consideration of multiple perspectives. Students now are being asked to demonstrate, in a significant way, what they know and are able to do. Rather than measuring discrete, isolated skills, authentic assessment emphasizes the application and use of knowledge.

Authentic assessment includes the holistic performance of worthwhile, complex tasks in challenging environments that involve contextualized problems. For example, the elementary teacher who plans for a student "invention convention" provides students with the authentic task of becoming an inventor. Use of a problem-solving model and rubrics for the process and product of inventing something will enable learners to see success in the task. In addition, both teachers and students can use the steps of the problem-solving model and the rubrics for assessment of the project. Using the specific evaluation criteria on the rubrics, it is not difficult to grade the project for report card purposes (see Chapter 10).

Authentic assessment must involve the examination of the process as well as the product of learning. Progress in both process and product can be measured by assessing parallel performances over time. In assessing the process and product of a student's writing, for example, friendly letters should be compared with friendly letters and not story writing. To evaluate a student's progress successfully, then, the teacher needs to collect similar products over time and apply the same criteria to all.

Both product and process assessment methods can be accurately and fairly assessed through the use of evaluation criteria. The criteria, however, must be specific enough that students understand what is expected of them. For example:

> *Vague Criterion: The poster should show elements of creativity.* Creativity is a term with multiple interpretations by most students. Some students will interpret this as colorful, others as "wild", while still others may think they need to produce an original, one-of-a-kind poster (a rather daunting task).
>
> *Specific Criterion: The poster should be eye-catching, causing the viewer to make a "double take".* Students can actually try the success of this criterion out on a variety of viewers. Posters are meant to attract attention and this criterion is specific to the task of designing a poster.

The specific criteria must also be known in advance by students so they can apply the criteria themselves as they work through the expected process to arrive at the desired product. Students as well as teachers can make formative assessments and continue or modify the work in progress. In the absence of clear, specific criteria explained in advance by the teacher, process and/or product assessment remains an isolated and incidental activity and the success of the learner is mostly left to chance.

Specific evaluation criteria also have a positive impact on instruction. Establishing the criteria before the instruction focuses the teacher on the critical components of the curriculum and increases the likelihood that instruction will emphasize such components. Thus, there is an integration and alignment of curriculum content, instruction, and assessment. Such integration and alignment procedures assist teachers and students alike to engage in meaningful learning.

CONSIDERING STUDENTS WITH SPECIAL NEEDS

The underlying principles of authentic assessment harmonize well with the movement to include learners with special needs into regular education classroom settings. The main difference in special education and regular education is the degree of individualization that is stressed in special education instruction. The learner-centered, relevant methods used in authentic tasks and assessments serve to increase the amount of attention paid to individual students. All teachers, including regular education teachers with inclusionary classrooms, who work with students with disabilities need a wide variety of information about their students; the more precise the information, the better. McLoughlin and Lewis (1998) wrote the following about the profound changes in the assessment and evaluation of all school students, including those with disabilities:

> A great deal of weight is being placed upon the outcome-based evaluation model as the basis for judging student performance, deciding whether schools and teachers are functioning appropriately, and even forcing fundamental changes in teaching methods and the structure of schools. The emphasis upon authentic assessment means that evaluation strategies are more functional, holistic, and contextual in terms of real-life performance. They incorporate the observation of groups of students solving a problem together, followed by individual student response activities and the evaluation of a variety of items arranged in a portfolio. (p. 6)

In addition, the Individuals with Disabilities Education Act (IDEA) Amendments of 1997 (Public Law 105–17) included several provisions that encourage general and special educators to use classroom-based assessments that link assessment, instruction, and evaluation. One assessment that accomplishes this linkage is portfolio assessment (Salend, 1998). The use of portfolios appears to be of particular interest to special educators because portfolios provide information for both the teacher and parents to help children question and reflect on their own work (Searfoss, Gelfer, & Bean, 1997). Portfolio assessment with the purpose of showing progress can provide the entire educational team with real and understandable signs that the student with special needs is learning.

Authentic assessment methods help us measure products, progress, and the process of learning and, at the same time, clearly communicate to students the standards for academic success in all areas. The communication of standards coupled with student reflection on their progress empowers students to become involved in their learning and increases the chance of producing quality work for all students.

Happily then, Ms. Ruiz, the first year teacher in the opening paragraph, should not change her instruction at all. To provide instruction in formats that closely resemble conventional tests because of a misalignment of instruction and assessment (reporting) would be detrimental to her students. She may, however, consider leading or serving on a committee to recommend report card changes to her school district that will include both conventional and authentic methods of assessment. In the meantime, she can augment the existing reporting system with evidence of student work toward specific evaluation criteria via completing rubrics on the many engaging projects and presentations enjoyed by her students. With the advent of the twenty-first century, creating lifelong learners and problem-solving adults should be the schools' major focus (Grady 1994). To accomplish this, Ms. Ruiz must encourage students to be engaged in their own learning, locate all necessary information, work cooperatively with other students, and produce high quality work.

The next chapter looks at how reform movements in education that recommend alternative forms of assessing student learning are impacting upon the core curricular areas. Instructional and assessment strategies in social studies, science, mathematics, and language arts will be considered in accordance with current statewide assessment changes.

HELPFUL INTERNET ADDRESSES:

www.ericae.net
ERIC Clearinghouse on Assessment and Evaluation

www.cec.sped.org
The Council for Exceptional Children, an international professional organization

www.504idea.org
The Council of Educators for Students with Disabilities

www.eskimo.com/~userkids.html
The Gifted Resources Home Page containing links to all online gifted resources and enrichment programs.

CHAPTER 2

Assessment Trends in the Core Subjects

*An American educator who was examining the British educational
system once asked a headmaster why so little standardized testing
took place in British schools. "My dear fellow," came the reply, "In
Britain we are of the belief that, when a child is hungry, the child
should be fed, not weighed.*

—Anonymous

The United States Department of Education (Baker, 1996) reported that preliminary observations of classroom instruction in Kentucky and Vermont, two states with portfolio assessment, indicate that teachers spend more time training students to think critically and solve complex problems than they did previously. After studying Vermont's portfolio assessment program during the first two years of its implementation, the RAND corporation concluded that the effects of portfolio assessment on instruction were substantial and positive (Koretz, 1994). Between seventy and eighty-nine percent of the math teachers reported more discussion of math, more explanation of solutions, and more writing about math in their classrooms since the advent of the portfolios. Pam Ladd and Sharon Hatton (1997) found that students in Kentucky are writing more and doing more group work as a result of the new state testing program and that, overall, student writing has become more expressive and imaginative. Clearly, the movement toward school reform via new assessment methods is a serious one that is soundly research-based.

It is not surprising, then, that national education associations are using the current research to advise teachers on the best ways to teach a particular content area and to recommend curriculum, instruction, and assessment methods to state departments of education. The following sections serve to give a content area review of what is suggested for the elementary area core curricular areas: social studies, language arts, science, and mathematics. Although they are listed separately, it is important to keep in mind that integrating curriculum around a central theme or concept is acknowledged to be the way in which students make lasting meaning from instruction.

THE SOCIAL STUDIES

According to the National Council for the Social Studies, the goal of social studies education is to promote civic competence in order to help students develop the ability to make informed and reasoned decisions for the public good. This goal does not seem particularly daunting until the vast amount of content in the social studies is considered. A few of the content areas subsumed within the social studies curriculum are economics, history, geography, political systems, culture, governance, and civics.

Just considering the huge amount of information contained in these subject areas makes it rather apparent that fixed response testing that asks students to demonstrate recall is a haphazard way, at best, to think about instruction and assessment in social studies. If elementary teachers were to engage in facts-based instruction which, in turn, was assessed with objective-style exams, then very little else would be accomplished all year long and the facts memorized would only be the tip of the iceberg. For example, a conventional test would ask students to match capital cities with their countries. An authentic assessment task would ask students to prepare a travel brochure that highlights travel to capital cities in a given geographic area (i.e., a tour of the Capital Cities of Eastern Europe). Such a task asks students to do much more than memorize the capital cities of countries. The students will need to explore the relationship of the countries and cities within a common geographic setting and use knowledge of the area so that "travelers" using the brochure will know important facts about the area, such as its history, government, and important attractions to visit. In light of the enormous amount of content knowledge that cannot be learned through rote instruction, it seems fair to say that nowhere in the curriculum is the need for nonconventional assessment stronger than in the social studies.

The National Council of Social Studies has assisted educators in moving from teaching facts to teaching concepts by publishing *Expectations of Excellence: Curriculum Standards for Social Studies* (Schneider, et al., 1994) for the teaching of social studies:

> The students will identify and use key concepts such as chronology, causality, change, conflict, and complexity to explain, analyze and show connections among patterns of historical change and continuity. (p. 34)

Such standards help teachers see the possibilities of integrating social studies into other areas of the curriculum. For example, constructing and reading graphs in mathematics can help students to observe and analyze change. An awareness of the natural environment in science can enable students to determine causality in economic decisions. In language arts instruction, good elementary teachers continually ask students to analyze and show connections among patterns found in a variety of stories and poems. But it is not enough to leave this planning for integration up to the teachers alone. School districts must provide the necessary support for curriculum developers and teachers to design the outcomes or frameworks from the National Council of Social Studies standards upon which instruction and assessment will be built.

For example, the New York State Framework for Social Studies (New York State Education Department, 1995) says, in part, that students will manage and organize data, make linkages between specific data and larger issues, view information from multiple perspectives, solve problems, and think clearly. Again, these are all skills and processes that can easily be integrated into other subject areas. Next, curriculum specialists and teachers select social studies content and develop activities and assessments that build upon the framework.

In Maryland, the Montgomery County Public Schools (1997) has determined grade level social studies outcomes for all elementary students. In addition, content, activities, and assessments were developed from these outcomes. Figure 2.1 gives a fifth-grade assessment task example with sample answers.

Such assessments ask students to use more complex and interrelated skills and knowledge such as how geography influenced economics in the American colonial period. These assessments influence and inform social studies instruction as well. Teachers will plan tasks and activities that foster a real-world application of skills such as conducting mock trials, preparing for and implementing point-counterpoint discussions and debates, and engaging students in community-based civic learning activities. These are a few of the many relevant and authentic activities found within the social studies curriculum that can easily become part of a portfolio for use during a thematic unit or as an end-of-the-school-year portfolio. Portfolio purposes and contents will be more thoroughly examined in Chapter 8 but a look at suggestions for a possible fifth grade end-of-the-year portfolio will help to see the quality of learning found in using authentic tasks. For example, Jones (1993) suggests the following contents of a fifth-grade portfolio:

1. A student self-assessment: What I have learned in fifth grade this year and what advice I would give to next year's students.

Just Imported from London

Activity 1

Step A: Select one type of colonial artisan trade and identify it on the line below. Based on the colonial artisan you selected, complete the chart below.

> **Sample Answer:** *Cooper*
> **Product(s) Made:** barrels, buckets, mugs
> **Skills the Artisan Needed:** woodworking skills so as not to waste materials, math for measuring and shaping tin to encircle the barrels.
> **Natural Resources the Artisan Needed:** wood, tin, fire, water
> **Capital Resources the Artisan Needed:** tools (pliers, hammer, measuring instruments), forge for tin

Step B: On the lines below, explain why the colonists needed or wanted the products you identified on the chart in Step A.

> **Sample Answer:** The colonists wanted barrels that coopers made to store and ship a lot of different products. They also wanted buckets made by coopers because they needed buckets for carrying water.

FIGURE 2.1   Fifth-grade assessment task with possible answers

2. Videotape or slide set with a cassette of a project (e.g., demonstration of a Native American craft).
3. A research project, such as "How People Make a Living in Argentina."
4. A draft of a story based on an Inuit tale or legend.
5. A summary of a group activity in which the student participated (e.g., a decision-making activity on each of five cities to visit: Toronto, Atlanta, San Diego, Caracas, and Rio de Janeiro).
6. A letter to a pen pal in another country, in which the student describes the characteristics of American culture.
7. A journal entry in which the student describes the advantages of democratic government.

The contents of this portfolio show the variety of tasks and activities that can be included in social studies assessment. Such assessment will provide teachers, students, and parents with information about the diverse ways students think and learn, the depth of their understanding, and the level of ability to use knowledge and skills.

SCIENCE

The *National Science Education Standards* (National Research Council, 1996) embrace the premise that science assessment is an integral part of the teaching process. According to the Standards, both instruction and assessment focus on the active search for knowledge or understanding to satisfy a curiosity that students have about the natural world. Research findings indicate that students are likely to begin to understand the natural world if they work directly with natural phenomena, using their senses to observe and using the tools of science to extend the power of their senses (National Science Board, 1991). This approach to teaching science is often called a "hands-on" method, which translates to elementary teachers that students will actively explore science understandings by using process skills such as observing, inferring, and experimenting.

The Science Standards add the idea of "minds-on" science by viewing inquiry as central to science learning. When engaging in inquiry, students describe objects and events, ask questions, construct explanations, test those explanations against current scientific knowledge, and communicate their ideas to others (National Research Council, 1996). Science education today requires a constructivist approach to teaching where teachers plan investigations that ask students to explore and categorize science concepts and restate concepts into relevant everyday situations (Ebenezer & Connor, 1998). The teaching of science and the assessment of science both emphasize active learning through student experimentation, reasoning, problem solving, and communicating regularly with other students and the teacher.

The changes in science assessment standards as recommended by the National Science Education Standards show a shift from conventional methods of assessment to more holistic methods (see Figure 2.2).

The new emphases conform to the premise of authentic assessment because such a shift in science assessment calls for exercises that closely approximate the intended outcomes of science education. Authentic assessment exercises require students to apply scientific knowledge and reasoning to situations similar to those they will encounter in the world outside the classroom, as well as to situations that approximate how scientists do their work.

The formats of science assessment are many and varied. For example, assessment possibilities can include performances, interviews, reports (both oral and written), journals, anecdotal records, student self-assessments, and portfolios. The contents of a science portfolio could be journal entries, taped discussions, reactions to new concepts, creative science work, and a letter to a friend explaining a science concept (Ebenezer & Connor, 1998). Haury and

Changing Emphases in Science Assessment

Less Emphasis on:	More Emphasis on:
Assessing what is easily measured	Assessing what is most highly valued
Assessing discrete knowledge	Assessing rich, well-structured knowledge
Assessing scientific knowledge	Assessing scientific understanding and reasoning
Assessing to learn what students do not know	Assessing to learn what students do understand
Assessing only achievement	Assessing achievement and opportunity to learn
End-of-term assessments by teachers	Students engaged in ongoing assessment of their work and that of others
Development of external assessments by measurement experts alone	Teachers involved in the development of external assessments

FIGURE 2.2   Changes in science assessment from the *National Science Education Standards* (National Research Council, 1996) p. 21

Rillero (1994) recommend science assessment that includes more frequent use of verbal explanations, using assessment strategies that incorporate performance tasks, developing observational checklists and scoring schemes as well as compiling portfolios of student work. Many types of science assessment use open-ended questions in order to gauge the level of conceptual understanding or ability to solve problems. McColskey and O'Sullivan (1993) modeled a point-system rubric to be used with open-ended questions (see Figure 2.3). A point-system rubric assigns points for certain features of the student's response.

Open-ended questions are often scored with this approach because points can reflect partial as well as full credit for a response. Students can use the information in the rubric to judge the quality of their own answer as well as to adjust their conceptual understanding. Such student self-reflection and self-correction help to empower students to become more self-directed. Self-directed learning is a goal of science education just as it is an essential part of authentic assessment; the ability to self-assess understanding of concepts is an important tool toward developing self-directed learners.

Point System Rubric

Task: Grade-three students were given appropriate measuring equipment and asked to find out if stirring makes any difference in how fast sugar cubes and loose sugar dissolve.

4 points: If the response states that both types of sugar dissolve faster when stirred, but loose sugar still dissolves faster than cubes

3 points: If the response indicates that stirring made a difference but doesn't describe the relative difference (that loose sugar still dissolves faster)

2 points: If the response describes the relative speed (loose sugar dissolves faster) but not the effects of the stirring or if the response just describes what happens (stirring makes sugar fall apart)

1 point: For incorrect responses

0 points: For no response

FIGURE 2.3   Point system rubric for judging response to open-ended questions

MATHEMATICS

Mathematics education also places an emphasis on student learning rather than student sorting and, as a result, a critical purpose of assessment is to inform teaching. Student learning is no longer narrowly defined as measurement of computational ability, but also includes understanding of concepts and the ability to engage in problem solving. A holistic rubric as found in Figure 2.4 could help teachers in assessing the problem-solving skills of their students.

Teachers are expected to plan instruction for and assess student knowledge, concept understanding, and the use of math content and process. In the National Council of Teachers of Mathematics (NCTM) draft of the *Principles and Standards for School Mathematics* (NCTM, 1998), student assessment is described as providing the clearest and most complete picture of what students know and are able to do. The methods to yield this type of outcome are varied as shown by the following as quoted from the draft of the *Standards 2000*:

> There are many options available to teachers for assessing mathematical learning, including selected-response quizzes, student-constructed responses and open-ended questions, performance tasks, observations, conversations, and portfolios. Although all of these methods are appropriate for classroom assessment, some lend themselves more readily to some types of learning goals over oth-

Problem-Solving Rubric

Skill	Level 4	Level 3	Level 2	Level 1
Understanding the Problem	Shows complete understanding of the problem and has insights beyond the problem	Shows complete understanding of the problem	Shows partial understanding of the problem, needs teacher assistance to clarify	Requires teacher assistance to understand the problem
Making a Plan	Develops sophisticated strategies and applies them within an effective plan	Independently chooses and applies appropriate strategies and applies them effectively	Shows evidence of plans and use of a strategy, which may or may not be applied effectively	Needs assistance to choose an appropriate strategy— applies a strategy such as "guess and check" in a random way
Solving the Problem	Provides a correct and complete solution; may show more than one way to solve the problem	Independently provides a correct and complete solution	Makes a minor math error leading to a wrong answer or incomplete solution	Gives incorrect solution even with direction; makes major math errors
Describing the Solution	Explains reasoning with clarity, coherence, and insight	Independently explains reasoning in a well-organized way with justifications	Gives an answer and begins to elaborate upon explanations with teacher assistance	Explains reasoning in a disorganized way that is difficult to follow

FIGURE 2.4   A sample of a problem-solving rubric

ers. Observations and conversations afford informal feedback, giving teachers insight into students' thinking and guiding the hundreds of decisions they make daily. Short-answer quizzes may illustrate if students can apply procedures, whereas complex performance tasks may focus on students' abilities to apply mathematics in

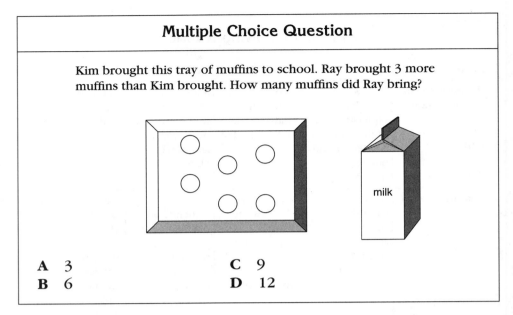

FIGURE **2.5**   Multiple choice question from the New York State Testing Program

new situations. Open-ended questions that ask students to explain how they arrived at their answers may reveal information about skills as well as conceptual understandings. Reflective journals can help teachers understand students' thinking and reasoning. (p. 38)

Clearly, the focus of mathematics assessment is much larger than the drill and practice instruction of old. Today's mathematics instruction is intricately linked to assessment and needs to include relevant problem-solving scenarios and authentic tasks that help students to reason and conceptualize mathematics.

The following examples of test items for fourth graders can be found in the *New York State Testing Program for Elementary and Intermediate Grades Information Brochure* (1997). They illustrate the different kinds of options available to teachers who practice a multimodal approach to math assessment. Figure 2.5 is an example of a multiple-choice question that asks the student to use information from a picture and from the text.

To solve this problem, the student must first select and then use the appropriate operation.

A short response question is presented in Figure 2.6. This item presents a problem that can be solved in several different ways. In this type of question, the student determines the solution by selecting the correct data, identi-

---

Short Response Question

Nick is going to mail some postcards. Each postcard costs 50¢ and each stamp costs 20¢.

Nick has $3.00 to spend on postcards and stamps. For every postcard he buys, he also needs to buy a 20¢ stamp. What is the greatest number of postcards he can mail?

Answer _____

Explain the mathematics you used to find your answer.

_____

_____

_____

_____

FIGURE 2.6   Example of a short response item from the New York State Testing Program

fying the mathematical requirements of the situation, and devising and ex-plaining a solution strategy.

An extended response item as shown in Figure 2.7 measures the students' ability to use data from a table to construct a bar graph with appropriate and consistent scales, title, and axis labels. The student is then asked to make a comparison based on his or her analysis of the data.

Clearly, elementary teachers of mathematics need to understand what students are thinking, how they approach problems, and what content they have learned. Teachers and students need a variety of assessment methods for gathering sufficient information to evaluate student learning and to inform teaching. In addition to conventional methods of assessment, student self-assessment and assessment of the process of learning will help teachers with evaluation in today's mathematics education.

LANGUAGE ARTS

Language arts represents the combination of reading, writing, listening, and speaking skills taught to students in elementary schools. Even with the differences in students, the availability of materials, and the variety of textbooks

Extended Response Question

The chart below shows the approximate length of a day on some of the planets in our solar system.

Planet	Length of Day (in hours)
Earth	24
Mars	25
Jupiter	10
Saturn	10

Part A

On the grid, make a bar graph showing the length of a day for each planet. Be sure to:

8. Title the graph
9. Label the axes
10. Include a correct number scale
11. Graph all the data

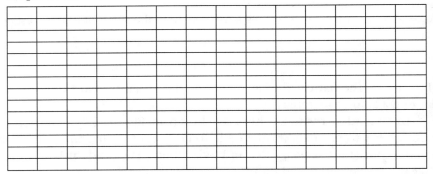

Part B

Using the data, write a statement comparing the length of a day on 2 or more planets.

_____

_____

_____

_____

_____

FIGURE 2.7   Extended response question from the New York State Testing Program

and tradebooks used in elementary classrooms today, elementary teachers agree that student success in language arts is a major instructional goal for all students. Teachers see language arts competency as valuable because it is needed for student learning in all other subjects and because language arts competency will prepare students for lifelong literacy demands. This common belief is reflected in the *Standards for the English Language Arts* (NCTE, 1996) when they say:

> Language is the most powerful, most readily available tool we have for representing the world to ourselves and ourselves to the world. Language is not only a means of communication, it is a primary instrument of thought, a defining feature of culture, and an unmistakable mark of personal identity. Encouraging and enabling students to learn to use language effectively is certainly one of society's most important tasks. (p. 1)

Recognizing that language arts is such an important instructional area and a large, complex one as well, the National Council of Teachers of English recommend that the current *Standards* (NCTE, 1996) serve as a point of discussion for school districts that are reviewing language arts curriculum, instruction, and assessment practices. Such discussions will help to tailor student outcomes to the particular needs of a school district.

The Jefferson County Public Schools in Golden, Colorado, had such a discussion that culminated in the formation of the English Language Arts Standards (1998) that follow:

Standard # 1: Students will read and understand a variety of materials.

Standard # 2: Students will read and recognize literature as an expression of human experience.

Standard # 3: Students will write effectively for a variety of purposes and audiences.

Standard # 4: Students will speak and listen for effective communication in a variety of contexts.

Standard # 5: Students will apply conventions of language for effective communication.

Standard # 6: Students will locate, evaluate, and use relevant information sources for their reading, writing, speaking, listening, and viewing.

Standard # 7: Students will apply complex thinking skills when reading, writing, speaking, listening, and viewing.

Standard # 8: Students will evaluate and improve the quality of their own reading, writing, speaking, listening, and viewing.

Instruction and assessment of these standards are best undertaken in a cross-disciplinary context and through a collaborative process between teachers and students.

Volumes have been written on how to assess language arts instruction and student learning. The use of teacher observation, checklists, a variety of criterion-referenced testing measures, rubrics, and student self-assessment all assess student learning in language arts. The point this book wishes to stress is that both instruction and assessment should be carried out in meaningful activities and settings. Interdisciplinary instruction can be responsive to children's curiosity and questions about real life. Such instruction can take advantage of the natural connections that cut across content areas and that are organized around questions, problems, or themes. The use of authentic assessment is especially valuable in classrooms using thematic, literature-based learning and texts of different difficulty levels (Weiner & Cohen, 1997). An example of a literature-based thematic unit can be found in Chapter 8.

Do classrooms exist that realize the instructional and assessment standards of the language arts? Yes they do and, while the environment might look different from classroom to classroom, they have many things in common. They are typically print-rich environments with a classroom research center, shelves of fiction and nonfiction tradebooks, and classroom access to the Internet. There is an instructional focus on asking questions arising from dissonance or curiosity and there is a system for student-led research and reporting on answers. Reading for pleasure is treasured and encouraged. Language arts lessons are taught all day, every day because language arts skills and attitudes permeate nearly everything learned and assessed in elementary schools. The following classroom vignette (NCTE, 1996) shows how the competencies in the English language arts standards can be realized in a lesson that asks students to analyze a short story:

> A class of students learns about characterization in fiction through reading Toni Cade Bambara's "Raymond's Run," a short story in which a young female protagonist comes to understand that competition and compassion cannot always coexist peacefully. The students begin by predicting the possible content of the story, based on the title, and they record these predictions (and their reasons for them) in their journals. The students listen to their teacher read the story aloud; then they read through selected passages themselves in small groups, stopping often to discuss their ideas or to write in their journals.
>
> After everyone has read the story, the teacher directs the students to write brief impressions of the story's protagonist, Squeaky, in their journals. The classmates exchange entries and discuss what

they have written, sharing their first impressions of the character. The class works as a whole to generate and discuss responses to questions their teacher has written, referring often to the text of the story to support their various responses.

Following this discussion, the teacher asks students to draw Squeaky as they visualize her, based on key passages they have chosen from the story. Then they make notes around their drawings, completing sentence starters provided by their teacher: "Squeaky likes . . . , Squeaky dislikes . . . , Squeaky sees the world . . . , Squeaky learns . . . ". They write the completed sentences around their drawing, like captions, and display their work for the class. After viewing one another's work and talking about what they have written, students write a more formal essay analyzing their responses to Squeaky's development as a character.

The students in this classroom are locating, evaluating and using relevant information sources for all the language arts components: reading, writing, listening, speaking, and viewing. They are practicing skills applicable to all subjects. In classrooms like this, students are learning how to learn.

Regardless of the subject area, assessment trends are moving toward application of information and skills. This greatly impacts on instruction as teachers will plan lessons that address products, process, and progress. Students will be able to construct meaning for themselves, reflect on the significance of the meaning, and self-assess to determine their own strengths and goals for improvement. In fact, instruction and assessment happen simultaneously in authentic assessment. The next chapter will show the benefits of aligning standards, instruction, and assessment.

HELPFUL INTERNET ADDRESSES:

www.nctm.org
The National Council of Teacher of Mathematics

www.ncte.org
The National Council of Teachers of English

www.ncss.org
The National Council for the Social Studies

www.ira.org
International Reading Association

www.nsta.org
The National Science Teachers Association

CHAPTER 3

Standards, Instruction, and Assessment

An education isn't how much you have committed to memory, or even how much you know. It's being able to differentiate between what you do know and what you don't.

Anatole France

In 1983 when the National Commission on Excellence in Education released the report, *A Nation at Risk,* educators, policy makers and American citizens in general were dismayed and alarmed to read the following:

> The educational foundations of our society are presently being eroded by a rising tide of mediocrity that threatens our very future as a nation and a people . . . We have, in effect, been committing an act of unthinking, unilateral educational disarmament. (p. 5)

During the years that followed this startling pronouncement, several changes have been made regarding curriculum and instruction. Scope and sequence charts that presented learning in a linear fashion were replaced by frameworks or standards that contain general statements of principles that allow some flexibility in what is taught and when it is to be learned (Hein & Price, 1994). This is not to say that a common elementary curriculum does not exist or that teachers can teach whatever they wish to teach. Rather, state curriculum guidelines with suggestions for implementation are formulated in every state department of education and disseminated to every school district across that state. Such guidelines encourage learning crossover from one content area to another and reflect the current movement toward active, integrated learning whether it is called thematic, constructivist, project-based, or hands-on/minds-on. How learning is assessed should match, or be aligned with, curriculum and instruction. So, the standards-based movement which grew out of *A Nation at Risk* (National Commission on Excellence in Education, 1983) determined that student outcomes will be improved through creating coherent systems of standards, instruction, and assessment.

CONCERNS WITH STANDARDS

Standards are important because they serve to clarify and raise expectations and because standards provide a common set of expectations (Kendall & Marzano, 1996). According to Marzano, Pickering, and McTighe (1993), standards are separated into two broad categories, content standards and lifelong learning standards. Content standards deal with the academic knowledge and skills belonging to a specific discipline. For example, two content standards for elementary school mathematics might be that students will understand the importance of shapes in our world and students will be able to recognize circles and squares. Lifelong learning standards deal with knowledge and skills that cut across all disciplines and are applicable to life outside the classroom (Marzano, et al.). Examples of lifelong learning standards in problem solving are that students will identify things that will help them solve a problem and express what they are thinking so that everyone can understand. Kendall and Marzano (1996) also include curriculum standards that describe overarching goals or the ways in which curriculum should be orchestrated to achieve a desired result.

There are problems, however, on the scope, purpose, and nature of standards. According to Kendall and Marzano (1996) a systematic effort must be made to remedy the following areas of concern, which can cause confusion in the selection of standards:

- multiple documents that state what students should know and be able to do; there needs to be a single comprehensive review so that states and schools can identify information important to them
- varying definitions of standards; content standards describe the knowledge and skills that students should attain, curriculum standards describe overarching goals, and lifelong learning standards that are applicable to life outside the classroom
- differing types of content description:
  - procedural as in *the learner is able to edit an essay*
  - declarative as in *the learner understands the conventions of punctuation*
  - contextual as in *the learner uses appropriate tone and style for a selected audience*
- differing grade ranges; benchmarks, or subcomponents of a standard, identify expected understanding or skill at various grade levels.

These are, by no means, insurmountable concerns. States and school districts that have addressed and resolved these concerns to their satisfaction have successfully chosen standards that have been appropriately aligned with instruction and assessment.

THE LINK BETWEEN STANDARDS, INSTRUCTION, AND ASSESSMENT

A careful selection of standards thus becomes a blueprint for what instruction will look like. In turn, the standards and instruction will determine methods of assessment that will then impact back on instruction and standards as pictured below:

$$\text{Standards} \leftrightarrow \text{Instruction} \leftrightarrow \text{Assessment}$$

Several states currently have an alignment of standards, instruction, and assessment in place. For example, Figure 3.1 lists examples of standards from the *Early Elementary Resource Guide to Integrated Learning*, a document from the University of the State of New York and the New York State Education Department (1997). These standards were developed by teachers, teacher educators, and members of the New York State Education Department as prescribed by the research on the need for active learning. State standards such as these are reflective of current research and are developmentally appropriate for the target level. State curriculum developers can then use the standards for a specific content area and develop curriculum guides with suggestions for implementation that may even include ideas for integrated thematic units of study.

Figure 3.2 illustrates some ways in which a particular standard is evident after implementation of lesson plans. More information about New York State standards can be found in the document *Early Elementary Resource Guide to Integrated Learning* (1997) as well as other documents from the New York State Department of Education. Frameworks and learning standards for other states can be found by contacting the state department of education in the capital city of a particular state.

Such evidence for student learning is, not so surprisingly, authentic. Students are being asked to *do* things that are found in real life. Using relevant, useful information to make graphs and charts, working cooperatively to engineer something, and designing working models of real devices all help to increase the chance of student success toward meeting the standards. Many school districts, upon receiving state standards and frameworks, form curriculum teams made up of teachers in order to develop ways in which all teachers in the district might plan instruction that incorporates the learning

A Sampling of Standards for Elementary Students

Standards for English Language Arts:

Standard 1. Students will read, write, listen, and speak for information and understanding.

Standard 3: Students will read, write, listen, and speak for critical analysis and evaluation.

Standards for Mathematics, Science, and Technology:

Standard 1: Students will use mathematical analysis, scientific inquiry, and engineering design as appropriate to pose questions, seek answers, and develop solutions.

Standard 4: Students will understand and apply scientific concepts, principles, and theories pertaining to the physical setting and living environment and recognize the historical development of ideas in science.

Standards for Social Studies:

Standard 2: Students will use a variety of intellectual skills to demonstrate their understanding of major ideas, eras, themes, developments, and turning points in world history and examine the broad sweep of history from a variety of perspectives.

Standard 3: Students will use a variety of intellectual skills to demonstrate their understanding of the geography of the interdependent world in which we live—local, national, and global—including the distribution of people, places, and environments over the Earth's surface.

Standards for the Arts:

Standard 2: Students will be knowledgeable about and make use of the materials and resources available for participation in the arts in various roles.

Standard 3: Students will respond critically to a variety of works in the arts, connecting the individual work to other works and to other aspects of human endeavor and thought.

FIGURE **3.1** Sampling of standards from the *Early Elementary Resource Guide to Integrated Learning*

Mathematics, Science, and Technology

Standard 1:   Students will use mathematical analysis, scientific inquiry, and engineering design, as appropriate, to pose questions, seek answers, and develop solutions.

This is evident, for example, when students:

- count the number of classmates whose birthdays occur in each month of the year; identify the month having the greatest, the least, as well as those months which have equal numbers of birthdays.
- estimate the size and number of building blocks that will be needed to construct a wall that will equal the height of a piece of classroom furniture.
- identify patterns for objects in the classroom and identify other objects in the school or community that have similar patterns.
- predict what will happen when red food coloring is added to play dough.
- observe how different insects move, and describe patterns of insect movement; compare and contrast these movements with other living things.
- work in small groups to plan a long-term project in an outdoor setting (e.g., garden, and nature trail) to observe and describe changes in animals, people, plants, and weather from season to season.
- design and make a device (e.g., weather vane) that indicates wind direction.
- design and make an animal pull toy with moving parts that imitate the movement of a particular animal.
- complete an electrical circuit given a lamp, clamps, wires, and a 1.5 volt dry cell.

FIGURE 3.2   Standards and evidence for student learning from the *Early Elementary Resource Guide to Integrated Learning* (p. 9).

stated in the standards. Such local curriculum guides help to empower teachers in taking charge of both what and how curriculum will be implemented in addition to how learning is assessed. Since the use of standards leads teachers to plan authentic tasks, then the use of authentic assessment methods naturally follows.

PUTTING IT ALL TOGETHER

Figures 3.3 and 3.4 reflect a Standards-Based Instruction Model developed and used by the Los Angeles Unified School District. Standards were selected, culminating tasks or assignments were agreed upon, and assessment criteria were established to evaluate student work on the culminating task or assignment. It

Language Arts Example

Standard: Students should be able to retell, make predictions, make inferences, and evaluate passages from culturally diverse literature and other reading materials.

Culminating Task/Assignment:

First Grade: Retell the story *Goldilocks and the Three Bears*

Third Grade: Write a paragraph in which you retell the main facts of a story that was read to you and tell what you think will happen next in the story.

Assessment

First Grade:

4. Restates accurately the story sequence; includes descriptions of main characters, conflict, outcomes, and setting; is confidently and clearly presented; uses rich vocabulary; requires no prompting.
3. Restates story sequence with minor errors; includes descriptions of main characters and some details of the conflict, outcomes, and setting; is clearly presented with minimal prompting.
2. Restates story sequence with some events omitted; includes descriptions of some of the main characters and a few details of the conflict, outcomes, and setting; is presented hesitantly and requires prompting for details and audibility.
1. Restates inaccurately the story sequence; mentions few characters; may not include descriptions of conflict, outcomes, or setting; is sometimes inaudible and needs prompting.

Third Grade:

4. Retells the main facts of the story; contains complete sentences; is legible; has an appropriate title.

3. Retells most of the main facts; is legible; uses complete sentences and has a title.

2. Misses many of the main facts; is generally legible; has a title which isn't quite appropriate.

1 May have one or two main facts but they are difficult to understand; uses many incomplete sentences; is not legible; does not give a title.

FIGURE 3.3   Language arts standards-based instruction model, Los Angeles Unified School District, Los Angeles CA

Science Example

Standard: The students should be able to identify the characteristics of living things, including humans, and how they interact with each other, and ways they adapt to their changing environment.

Culminating Task/Assignment

Kindergarten: Talk about how living and nonliving things act upon one another and how they change their ways in a terrarium. Participate in a final interview.

Third Grade: Create a diorama that depicts the plant and animal life found in a particular ocean environment. Make a presentation to explain the food web for the plants and animals in the diorama.

Assessment

Kindergarten:

4. Identifies living things and nonliving things in the terrarium, how they interact with each other, and what changes they make.

3. Identifies most living things and nonliving things in the terrarium, how they interact with each other, and some changes they make.

2. Identifies only a few living things and nonliving things in the terrarium, how they interact with each other, or change they make.

1. Does not identify living things and nonliving things in the terrarium, how they interact with each other, or changes they make.

Third Grade: Both the diorama and the presentation:

4. Identify the characteristics of living and nonliving things found in the ocean; explain their interactions and adaptations depending on the area of the ocean chosen; present information logically and clearly.

3. Identify the characteristics of living and nonliving things but may not explain all of their interactions and adaptations correctly; present available information logically and clearly.

2. Do not identify some characteristics of living and nonliving things; do not explain most interactions and adaptations; present information in an unclear way.

1. Do not identify most characteristics of living and nonliving things; include few animals or plants; do not explain interactions or adaptations.

FIGURE 3.4 Science standards-based instruction model, Los Angeles Unified School District, Los Angeles, CA

is important to note the differing grade-level tasks and assessments on the same standard.

It is readily apparent that the assessment components of this standards-based model can easily be labeled a rubric. As defined in Chapter 1, a rubric is an assessment device that uses clearly specified evaluation criteria and proficiency levels that measure student achievement of those criteria. The criteria provide descriptions of each level of performance in terms of what students are able to do. Figure 3.4 shows an example of a standards-based model in science.

An assessment rubric can easily be drawn from any subject in this standards-Based Instruction model. Figure 3.5 shows a kindergarten, level rubric from the above science example. Given that the teacher, planned, and implemented activities that enabled students to knowledgeably discuss how living and nonliving things act upon one another and how they change their ways in a terrarium setting, those students can be assessed on the standard through the use of a holistic rubric. A holistic rubric gives an overall evaluation of student work without analyzing the strengths or weaknesses of each

---

Interview Rubric

Standard: The students should be able to identify the characteristics of living things, including humans, and how they interact with each other, and ways they adapt to their changing environment.

Rating Description of Response

4   Identifies living things and nonliving things in the terrarium, how they interact with each other, and what changes they make.

3   Identifies most living things and nonliving things in the terrarium, how they interact with each other, and some changes they make.

2   Identifies only a few living things and nonliving things in the terrarium, how they interact with each other, or changes they make.

1   Does not identify living things and nonliving things in the terrarium, how they interact with each other, or changes they make.

Feedback on student response:

_____

_____

_____

FIGURE **3.5**   Holistic rubric for kindergarten science standard

part of the work separately. The section that requires the teacher to give specific feedback on the student response provides an analysis on the distinct parts of the answer and on the individual student's quality of response.

Thus, standards serve to furnish educators with a common language and as a guide for curricular decisions by providing common learning expectations essential for all students. These learning expectations, or standards, can address the knowledge, processes, and attitudes of students. The standards-based curricular decisions, in turn, provide ideas for both instruction and assessment that contribute to meeting the standards for all children.

All national professional organizations have developed clear, coherent standards for students in grades kindergarten through twelve in all subject areas. These standards can be found most readily on the Internet sites of the professional organizations such as the National Council for the Social Studies, the National Council for Teachers of Mathematics, the National Council for Teachers of English, and the National Science Teachers Association to name a few. These organizations all recommend the use of authentic assessment methods to measure many of their standards. The next chapter will illustrate the nature of meaningful authentic tasks that are often present in standards-based instructional models.

HELPFUL INTERNET ADDRESSES:

www.totalreading.com
This site contains K–6 Reading/Language Arts curricula

www.cse.ucla.edu/CRESSTHome.html
CRESST, the Center for Research on Evaluation, Standards, and Student Testing

www.mcrel.org
Mid-continent Research for Education and Learning containing standards for all content areas

www.putwest.boces.org/standards.html
An annotated list of Internet sites with K–12 educational standards and curriculum framework documents

CHAPTER 4

Meaningful Authentic Tasks

I hear and I forget.

I see and I believe.

I do and I understand.

—Confucius

Today one rarely sees elementary students silently sitting in rows, all passively doing the same work. Now teachers prefer tables to desks, students are working at integrated, thematic learning centers and learning is much more active and individualized. Teachers arrange classrooms and plan for instruction after carefully considering the learning styles of their students. The arrangement of furniture, the use of student-generated decorations, and the tone of discussion used in the classroom will influence the kind of learning that takes place in elementary classrooms (Kohn, 1996). A movement from teacher-centered classrooms to learner-centered classrooms is taking place. The primary goal in today's typical elementary classroom is to improve student learning, not student test scores

Although many classrooms reflect differences in teaching style and use of resources, there are many common factors among elementary classroom situations. Students are actively engaged in the learning process. Teachers plan for integrated instruction. Content in the core subject areas such as mathematics, social studies, science, and language arts are interwoven within a common theme so that students see the interrelationships among concepts and skills about which they are learning. Students are engaged in problem-solving and critical thinking activities. Authentic tasks are very much a part of the regular planning of today's teachers. This chapter will present some examples of authentic tasks and begin to look at ways to assess such tasks.

EXAMPLES OF AUTHENTIC TASKS

An authentic task is complex and will simulate important real-world challenges. It requires higher levels of cognitive thinking such as problem solving and critical thinking. Such tasks are important learning tasks because they focus on how knowledge can be found and used rather than simply acquiring knowledge. Students need to use their new knowledge in the everyday world in order to know it truly. They need to have the opportunity to make decisions with real consequences, which is what authentic tasks do for students (Nickell, 1993).

In a typical elementary classroom, authentic tasks are quite common and not nearly as intimidating as they sound. Good elementary teachers plan active lessons that ask students to plan, research, and think. Project work, for example, often includes some of the following authentic product outcomes:

- writing a brochure
- making a map
- creating a recipe
- writing and directing a play
- critiquing a performance
- communicating a message in a poster format
- inventing something useful
- producing a video
- creating a model
- writing a children's book
- making a computer program

These are only a few tasks that match important real-life tasks that are commonly planned and assigned by teachers.

The following additional examples of authentic tasks are intended to extend the kind of creativity found in elementary teachers who are good at designing lessons where students are asked to apply knowledge or information. They are meaningful tasks that parallel activities students will likely encounter in the real world and are easily modifiable for a variety of difficulty levels:

1. *Shopping for Surprises*
   Select a catalog of interest to people your age. Pretend that you have been given $250.00 to spend on surprise gifts for six friends. List each friend's name and then select a gift for each from the catalog. Remember that you have only $250.00 to spend so you will have to

shop carefully to make your money come out evenly, including shipping and handling for each purchase. You must either spend the entire $250.00 or have no more than $2.57 left over.

2. *Restaurant Birthday Party*

Plan a birthday party for yourself and five friends at a restaurant. Use the restaurant's menu to choose a complete meal that will be served to all six of you. Determine the cost of each meal. Determine the total amount of the bill, including your local sales tax and a fifteen percent tip.

3. *Meteorologist*

Keep a five-day record of precipitation and temperature for any five cities in the United States. Choose cities in different regions of the country. Record and graph the results. The graph can be in any form of your choice. Use a different color for each city so that the graph is easily readable.

4. *Pet Caregiver*

You will be given a Rabbit Care Guidebook that contains information about real rabbits. Your teacher will help you read this book. Then pretend that your teacher is giving a rabbit to your class as a pet. Using the information in the book, make a shopping list of things you need to buy in preparation for the rabbit's arrival.

5. *Community Journalist*

For the upcoming assembly, research information on the performance, take notes as you attend the event, and interview other people who attended the performance to solicit their opinion. Then write an article about the event that is suitable for publication in the community (or school) newspaper.

6. *Budding Audubons*

Collect seeds from all over and create a project to identify as many as possible of the plants from which the seeds are collected. Draw, photograph, or collect pictures of the plants and label them. Mount the results for display.

7. *Flight Contest for Engineers*

Build as many airplanes from scrap paper as you like. You may work alone or with others. Experiment with design and the use of paper clips to see which airplanes do best for different flight categories such as distance, flight time, and stunt flight. You or your group may submit planes for test flights in these categories.

It is not difficult for elementary teachers to work collaboratively in grade-level meetings to brainstorm authentic tasks such as these. The possibilities of subject area integration are clear to elementary teachers who have an understanding of the linkages in the elementary school curriculum. In fact, teachers can create units of study that are quite complex in nature. Subsequent examples will show how complex tasks can deepen learning and, at the same time, be evaluated fairly.

THE GROCERY STORE

The simulated grocery store in the elementary grades asks students to shop, make change, and consider the importance of nutrition, all in an authentic setting that transfers quite readily to the students' local convenience store. The grocery store center usually has empty food boxes, pictures of produce and cans with prices marked on them, a shopping cart, a toy cash register or calculator and realistic-looking, fake money. Two roles can be played at this center, the shopper and the shopkeeper. The specific duties of the shopper might be to purchase a well-balanced lunch for four people when given a limited amount of money. The job of the shopkeeper could be to open the store on time, to keep the shelves stocked and tidy, and to give correct change. Students would have a chance to play both roles according to a rotation schedule established by the teacher.

The complexity of the task becomes apparent when the learning outcomes from the grocery store center are noted. For example, students will practice the skills of estimating, adding, subtracting, and making change—all in a meaningful context. Students will develop a concrete understanding of weights and measurements, they will apply knowledge of nutritional requirements, and they will engage in problem solving with the aid of a calculator. The grocery store center has many variations among elementary teachers and is often planned as a school supplies store, a healthy snack shop, or other ideas relevant to students. Modifications to the center are made according to the grade level and skill levels of students. For example, the prices can be changed for easy computation.

The authentic nature of the task is attractive to students and teachers alike. In addition, the complexity of assessing student success in the task need not be daunting. In fact, authentic assessment methods will help to take the mystery out of assessment for students and increase the chance of producing quality work. Figure 4.1 shows a typical planning sheet for students playing the role of shopper.

As the students proceed through the task and apply knowledge from previous lessons and experiences, the chance to reflect on their work is very important. When students know exactly what is expected of them at the beginning of a task and are given the chance to self-reflect, they can then make modifications and adjustments as they proceed through their work. Figure 4.2 shows a self-reflection rubric that clearly indicates the evaluation criteria that will be used by the teacher.

Lunch for Four

You have $10.00 and need to shop for a nutritious lunch for four people. Consider our lessons on nutrition and the food pyramid as you plan. Use a calculator to determine real costs.

1. Predict what you think you can buy for lunch. Estimate the total costs.

Item	*How Many*	*Price estimate*
_____	_____	_____
_____	_____	_____
_____	_____	_____
_____	_____	_____

2. Revised shopping list after visiting store.

Item	*How Many*	*Actual Price*
_____	_____	_____
_____	_____	_____
_____	_____	_____
_____	*Total Price*	_____

3. How much change did you receive? Was it correct?

   Check: $10.00

   − Total Price

   Change back

4. Write a short paragraph to explain why you think your lunch is nutritious. Be sure to include information on the food pyramid. Remember to indent the first line in the paragraph and use a topic sentence with supporting details.

   _____

   _____

   _____

   _____

5. Complete the self-assessment rubric. Staple this worksheet to the rubric and put both in the work collection box.

FIGURE 4.1   Planning worksheet for shoppers

Shopper's Self-reflection Rubric

Directions: Please consider your work carefully. Complete the rubric in a thorough manner.

1. A complete lunch for four was planned.

            Yes   No   Somewhat

Comments _____

_____

2. The lunch was nutritious and uses correct information from our lessons on the food pyramid.

            Yes   No   Somewhat

Comments _____

_____

3. The paragraph on nutritional aspects had correct information and was well written (first line indented, topic sentence, supporting details).

            Yes   No   Somewhat

Comments _____

_____

4. Total price calculation was correct.

               Yes   No

5. Change received was checked correctly.

               Yes   No

6. Additional information: How and why did your prediction change after you went shopping? Also, reflect on what you would modify about this shopping experience if you were to do this again.

_____

_____

_____

_____

_____

FIGURE 4.2   Self-reflection rubric

The grocery store center now becomes more than having students play store. The teacher has predetermined what learning really matters in this task and what learning is reflective of lessons being taught to students. Students get to apply learning to a task that has a utilitarian purpose. Students and the teacher evaluate the quality of student achievement using multiple criteria in the form of clearly written standards that permit judgments of "better" or "worse". In addition, the use of student self-reflection helps the teacher to see the process experienced by individual students.

LETTER OF RECOMMENDATION

Intermediate-level elementary students know that the rewards of good character, useful work habits, and dependability will contribute to their success in school. They know that they will need good recommendations from teachers and other people who know them well in order to apply for a job or continued schooling. Lessons on identifying positive work habits and character traits are regularly taught in every elementary school. Writing for a purpose is also part of every elementary language arts curriculum. The next example of an authentic task combines the capability of students to perceive the character traits of a literary character with the skill of writing a letter of recommendation for that person.

Cathleen Deery is a fifth-grade teacher who has just completed a unit on the book *The Adventures of Tom Sawyer*. Considerable time was spent on identifying the traits of characters in the book and supporting selected traits with the actions and decisions made by the characters. In order to assess individual student learning, Ms. Deery planned a simulation where she played the role of a visiting principal, Livy Langdon, from a private elementary school. The students played the role of people who were asked to write a letter of recommendation for one of several applicants to the school, all of whom were characters in *The Adventures of Tom Sawyer*. All students were given the elements of a letter of recommendation to guide them in their work (see Figure 4.3).

The "principal" reviewed desirable character traits for students in her school, Mark Twain Elementary. She spoke of the importance of providing an honest appraisal of applicants as well as providing the reader with specific details to support the appraisal. Figure 4.4 is the rubric given to the students so they could monitor their success as a recommendation writer as they worked. Ms. Deery, as the principal, discussed the rubric with students before they completed the task.

Each criterion on the rubric was the focus of lessons taught by Ms. Deery. Students were asked to engage in peer review as they wrote in order to check on their progress toward meeting the criteria. When the final product

Elements of a Letter of Recommendation

Date
Return Address

Principal's Name

Address of School

Greeting

Introductory Paragraph

Supporting Paragraphs

Conclusion

Salutation

FIGURE 4.3   Elements of recommendation letter

Letter of Recommendation Rubric

Criteria	1	2	3
Each trait is supported by at least *two* actions or decisions made by selected character.	Highly demonstrated	Adequately demonstrated	Poorly demonstrated
Correct letter format is used.	Highly demonstrated	Adequately demonstrated	Poorly demonstrated
Correct mechanics are used (spelling, usage, grammar).	Highly demonstrated	Adequately demonstrated	Poorly demonstrated
Writing is fluent. Letter is easily understood.	Highly demonstrated	Adequately demonstrated	Poorly demonstrated

Specific feedback and comments:

_____

_____

_____

FIGURE 4.4   Rubric for letter of recommendation

(the letter) was submitted to Ms. Deery, she used the rubric to complete her evaluation of the letter. Specific feedback presented evidence for the scores marked by Ms. Deery and comments helped students to make goals for improvement in future products involving both character traits and letter writing skills.

FOOD SERVICE WORKER

This next example shows an authentic task that does not need a rubric for evaluation purposes. As part of a nutrition unit, Merrie King asked her students to pretend they were food service workers whose task it was to determine the kinds and amounts of foods to buy for school lunches. Students collected a week's worth of classroom data about lunch choices and were then asked to demonstrate their understanding of writing mathematical equations that were based on the data (see Figure 4.5).

Ms. King then asked the students to answer the following questions.

1. Using the class lunch chart, write a math problem showing how many students had a regular school lunch this week.
2. Using the chart, write a math problem showing how many students had peanut butter and jelly sandwiches this week.

School Lunch Chart

Lunch	Monday	Tuesday	Wednesday	Thursday	Friday
Regular	Mac & Cheese 7	Pizza 20	Cheeseburger 5	Grilled Cheese 12	Tacos 8
Meat and Cheese	3	0	1	2	4
Peanut Butter and Jelly	5	2	3	6	3
Tuna	5	1	5	0	2
Brought From Home	5	2	11	5	8

FIGURE 4.5 School lunch chart

3. How many more meat and cheese sandwiches were ordered this week than peanut butter and jelly sandwiches?
4. Write a math problem showing how many school lunches (including sandwiches) were ordered on Monday and Tuesday.
5. Write a math problem showing how many more school lunches were ordered Monday and Tuesday than were brought from home.
6. Looking at the lunch chart, which type of lunch do most students order? How do you know? Why do you think this is so?
7. Which kind of lunch do you think most students will order next week? Why do you think so?

While there are a variety of ways to write correct equations, there is still only one correct answer. For example, correct student responses for question # 4 could look like Figure 4.6, depending on how the student organized the data (see Figure 4.6):

An assessment of the student's thinking can be easily made as the teacher checks the equations. In cases of doubt, the teacher can interview the student in order to determine the way the student thinks about the problem. The teacher can then plan additional lessons based on the students' needs as determined by the assessment that looks at 1) the right answer and 2) the method of arriving at an answer. The task is an authentic task because it asks students to do what people do in real life. However, it does not require a rubric because the proficiency levels are simply "the answer is correct" or "the answer is incorrect". The process at arriving at an answer is easily observable by the teacher and the teacher can readily prepare for remediation if necessary. A journal entry could also be assigned using a prompt that asks students to explain what they were thinking as they solved the

---

#4. Write a math problem showing how many school lunches (including sandwiches) were ordered on Monday and Tuesday.

$$7 + 3 + 5 + 5 + 20 + 2 + 1 = 43$$

or

$$20 + 23 = 43$$

or

$$10 + 10 + 20 + 3 = 43$$

FIGURE 4.6   Possible correct student responses

problem. The most recent discussion draft of the *Principles and Standards 2000 for School Mathematics,* released by the National Council of Teachers of Mathematics (NCTM, 1998) recommends including practice with problems that look at both algorithmic responses and written samples in which students tell about the process of solving the problem. This serves the dual purpose of assisting students in self-reflection as well as influencing and informing teaching.

ADDING AUTHENTICITY VIA THE INTERNET

Part of planning for authentic instruction includes taking inventory of the resources available that help to add authenticity to instruction. Websites on the Internet can often do that and, of course, must be carefully reviewed for suitability and usability much in the same way teachers review any resource intended for instructional use. Lisa Howell from Forty Fort, Pennsylvania, planned a unit of study for fourth graders on the culture of ancient Egypt. Her goals and objectives for the unit included investigation in how modern day archaeologists discovered and literally uncovered ancient Egypt. She wanted her students to understand the goals and the work of archaeologists so that students could generalize this information to the future study of any culture.

One of the activities Lisa planned included an archaeological dig using workstations in the classroom (see Figure 4.7). Before students began their own authentic task of doing the work of an archaeologist, Lisa planned for groups of students to "take an Odyssey in Egypt" by using the Website at *http://www.scriptorium.org/odyssey* that contains photographs and interesting text to help students feel that they are a part of an actual archaeological dig in Egypt. Lisa extended this visual trip to Egypt with an archaeological dig right in the classroom.

Ms. Howell states that the students' interest level, knowledge, and purpose for learning was clearly enhanced by using the Odyssey in Egypt Website. Several students found additional sites on their own to explore and research answers to questions that emerged from their classroom work.

There are numerous websites to help teachers and students meet curricular goals and objectives. In fact, there are several "WebQuests" that contain integrated units of study common to elementary curricula and that are contained right on the WebQuest. A WebQuest is an inquiry-oriented activity in which most or all of the information used by learners is drawn from the web. The WebQuest model was developed by Bernie Dodge with Tom March in 1995 at San Diego University. School districts should provide teachers with the time and direction to explore and review these websites for use in their daily and long-range planning. Examples of WebQuests can be found at *http://www.users.massed.net/~mdurant/AncientEgyptWebquest.com*

Authentic Task: Archaeological Dig

You are an archaeologist. You have been asked to join a team of archaeologists in Egypt. They are digging up some interesting things!

Around the classroom you will find workstations that represent a piece of land in Egypt. Your job is to uncover any artifacts that may be buried there. Record your findings on the data collection sheet provided.

These are the steps that you need to follow:
1. *Secure your site and gather your clues.* Using the materials provided, rope off your site and record any evidence you find on the surface.
2. *Excavate your workstation.* Using the tools provided, excavate. As you dig, keep your area as level as possible. If you dig holes, you might damage evidence. Record any evidence you find as you dig through the levels of soil. *Important:* If you find pottery pieces, put them into a small pail and wash with water and a soft brush. Remove the pieces from the water and let them dry.
3. *Make a drawing of your workstation.* Label your evidence (what is it? where did you find it?)
4. *Report your findings.* When you complete digging and all of your evidence is uncovered, the site needs to be documented through a report of any problems encountered and the materials and procedure used.
5. *Interpretation of Evidence:* Once all of your evidence is collected, you need to figure out what it means. Repair your artifact and identify what you have found. What do you think the ancient Egyptians used this artifact for and why do you think as you do?

FIGURE 4.7   Authentic task: archeological dig

(Ancient Egypt Webquest) and *http://www.plainfield.k12.in.us/hschool/ webq/webq8/jjquest.htm* (Simple Machines WebQuest). The Internet can be a useful tool for adding an authentic nature to instructional tasks and teachers need the time to adequately review sites for appropriateness.

As authentic tasks are included in elementary school instruction, teachers will become facilitators of student understanding by asking students to *use* knowledge by *doing* tasks. Such student engagement with learning is what Confucius meant by "I do and I understand". The next chapter will look at the value of rubrics for teachers and students, especially for the teacher who regularly plans complex authentic tasks and feels uncomfortable assessing them.

HELPFUL INTERNET ADDRESSES:

http://www.ericir.syr.edu/Virtual/Lessons
This site contains over 1,000 lesson plans that have been written by teachers all over the United States

http://www.kn.pacbell.com/wired/bluewebn
A library of Blue Ribbon learning sites on the web that feature lesson and unit plans by subject

http://www.awesomelibrary.org
This site organizes the web with 14,000 carefully reviewed resources including the Top 5 Percent in Education

http://www.edweb.sdsu.edu/webquest/webquest.html
The WebQuest home page with lots of web-based units

CHAPTER 5

Common Assessments and Rubrics

Thirty years ago when I first began teaching, the curriculum seemed to be determined by the textbooks selected for each grade level. My students, whom everyone seemed to have given up on, were "disadvantaged" (from the projects) and teaching from the book bored and frustrated them to no end. In order to prevent impending chaos and to give them something relevant to do, I set up a cooking station in the classroom. Groups of four students were asked to pool their lunch money every week and plan a nutritious lunch for four that they could eat in our classroom. They could also invite a fifth person to join them, which seemed to add to the seriousness of their efforts (company's coming!). They learned that shopping at the local convenience store would net them half the amount of food than the Giant supermarket and that the "junk" we were learning in health class and math might have some relevancy to their lives.

Last year, when I attended an inservice program on authentic assessment, I thought back on our cooking station and thought about how much more those kids could have learned. Rubrics on products, progress, and process would have helped to make learning via cooking a really powerful experience for my students and me.

Clarence Washington
5th grade teacher

D uring the time when measurement of learning was quantifiable, the widespread use of objective tests such as multiple choice, matching, fill-in-the-blank, and true/false provided teachers with a reliable, easy-to-score means of evaluating student retention of information. In fact, considerable test theory and statistical techniques were developed at this time to support the development and use of such tests. For decades, testing and measurement classes in teacher education schools taught prospective teachers how to construct such tests in accordance with the statistical standards set by test reliability and validity. Report cards began to reflect these numerical standards as well with the advent of percentage grades.

It is not surprising that the ease with which this rote assessment system could be administered was appealing to most teachers. It was an efficient way to give tests and tests were easy to score. In addition, with such "precision of measurement", a percentage score of 82 on a report card was difficult for a student to dispute, especially when it was a result of the student's ability to memorize. There was no room for discussion about a grade when there was one, and only one, possible correct answer to a question. This narrow band of testing led to an equally narrow band of instruction. Subjects in elementary school were taught in isolation with a time for mathematics, reading, social studies, and so on. Learning was regarded as a great many facts to learn with little or no integration among subjects. When one is measuring information, then one first has to give information. Thus began many years of information dissemination by teachers to students with students showing rote memory ability via an objective test score.

With the advent of the knowledge explosion and the technology that allows us to access enormous quantities of information, such a memory-based curriculum seemed outdated and obsolete. Surely, the sole goal of giving knowledge level information to students would not be acceptable in today's world. Our beliefs about learning have changed. For example, early theorists who were supporters of a knowledge-based approach to learning saw the learning of basic skills by rote as an essential first task of students. After the basic skills were learned, it was erroneously assumed that students could automatically use the basic skills to build complex understandings and perceptions.

In fact, learning does not proceed by the accumulation of a common set of basic skills but can follow multiple strategies and pathways (O'Malley & Pierce, 1996). Teachers who insist on facts before thinking are definitely in the minority and would benefit from in-service education on current learning theory. Such teachers often argue that the delivery of content precedes reasoning about that content and that "covering" content is such an enormous task in itself, the development of understanding will have to wait. Learning is much less linear than this and much more active. Content is learned by reasoning, and understanding is developed as students interact with information that covers the field of study (Mills-Courts & Amiran, 1994). Students who have understood and can use previous information in an active and critical way are those who acquire further knowledge.

Findings from current cognitive psychology indicate that learning requires that the learner engage in thinking while actively constructing meaningful schema (Gagne, Yekovich, & Yekovich, 1993). To learn something is not just to have taken in information, but to have interpreted it and related it to other knowledge one already has. The best teachers plan lessons that ask children to use information so that meaningful schema can be constructed. For example, elementary teachers use cognitive research as they develop integrated thematic units of study that feature problem-solving and critical-thinking activities. Such planning helps to individualize instruction and learning by providing multimedia resources with a variety of difficulty levels so all children are able to complete the activities.

The primary task of teachers, therefore, is to use strategies that cognitively engage students while assisting students to use the vast amount of information resources available to students and teachers. Elementary teachers are no longer in the business of solely teaching "what" is to be learned, but also must teach "how" we learn in this age of information overload.

COMMON PRACTICES

Some teachers incorrectly assume that the authentic assessment movement implies an end to conventional forms of teacher-made tests such as multiple choice, short answer, and true/false tests (Marzano, Pickering, & McTighe, 1993). These kinds of tests are still powerful assessment devices, particularly for measuring the correctness of factual content information. Authentic assessment is not meant to replace conventional testing, but rather to add to the multifaceted approach of contemporary assessment. In fact, multiple choice, true/false, matching, short answer, and essay tests can be effective tools for assessing students' understanding of declarative content simply because they are highly focused (Marzano, et al.). Such tests, however, do not tap many of the skills and abilities that students need to develop in order to be successful in later schooling and in life. As previously stated, conventional standardized testing yields limited measures of learning and narrows the curriculum. Moreover, conventional testing fails to tap both higher-order skills and students' abilities to perform real-world tasks (Resnick, 1987). Conventional testing is still an important piece of the total assessment pie, but there are many other pieces of the pie as well.

Decisions about how to best assess students' understanding are complex and may require the use of multiple indicators of performance (Azwell & Schmar, 1995). According to Azwell, only recently have the assessment and evaluation systems begun to change to reflect our new understanding of the learning continuum and the implementation of a broader range of instructional strategies. In addition to conventional objective test measures, teachers now seek information about a student's learning in an ongoing, multifaceted approach that includes observations of processes and products and student self-evaluations. Criterion-referenced tests, teacher-made tests, contract grading, and interviews are some of the means of accessing such information. Wildemuth (1984) defines these methods of assessment as follows:

- *criterion-referenced tests*

  Criterion-referenced tests are designed to evaluate the accomplishment of specifically stated instructional objectives. They may resemble norm-referenced tests in format and in type of administration and scoring. They differ in the way they are interpreted. Criterion-referenced assessment tells teachers how well students are performing on specific goals or standards rather than just telling how their performance compares to a norm group of students nationally or locally. In this way, criterion-referenced tests can be more useful to teachers in identifying and planning remedial instruction in the areas in which an individual student or the entire class has demonstrated weaknesses.

- *teacher-made tests*

  Teacher-made tests are advocated because they can be tailored to specific curricula or specific needs for information about students. Generally, teacher-made tests are criterion referenced and are designed to measure students' mastery of the material being taught. They can provide information on small units of instruction not covered by standardized tests.

- *contract grading*

  In a contract grading system, the teacher and student agree at the beginning of a unit on particular course objectives to be fulfilled by the student, on the support to be provided by the instructor, and on how the results will be evaluated. The contract provides a form of record keeping that documents student achievement in relation to specified objectives. Upon completion of a contract, teacher and student cooperatively evaluate the work, choose new assignments, and seek to clarify previous or newly stated objectives. One caution is in order: a contract should be used as a process for learning rather than merely an instrument for getting a job done.

- *interviews*

  Interviews with students and parents can also yield information useful in evaluating the student's progress. An interview with a student can be as specific as a teacher sitting with a child and asking him or her to share information about how to solve particular mathematics problems. Or it may be broad and probe classroom activities, student-peer interaction, classroom problems, and teacher and school goals. Parent interviews may yield unique ways of looking at the child's progress for both the teacher and the parents. (p.1)

These are but a few of the ways in which elementary teachers assess student learning. When students are engaged in the kinds of authentic tasks found in Chapter 4, rubrics can add to the total assessment process.

HOW RUBRICS CAN HELP

As defined in Chapter 1, a rubric is an assessment device that uses clearly specified evaluation criteria and proficiency levels that measure student achievement of those criteria. The criteria used in rubrics are necessary conditions that must be met for the outcomes to be realized successfully. The criteria provide descriptions of each level of performance in terms of what students are able to do. Specific evaluation criteria help to distinguish between quality work and inferior work. The criteria are known in advance by students and, in some cases, students may have assisted in developing the criteria.

When selecting and describing the criteria for a task, Piccolo and Younghans (1994) suggest that the teacher consider the following steps:

- Step 1: Determine the focus of the assessment. What exactly is the task and what significant knowledge, skills, and processes should students demonstrate to be successful?
- Step 2: Determine how many categories are necessary to describe the knowledge, skills, and processes associated with the task.
- Step 3: Describe the specific observable actions and processes that would indicate success in the task.
- Step 4: Determine how many levels of performance are appropriate for the task.
- Step 5: Determine the format.

Teachers and/or students, depending on the assessment objectives, can score rubrics. Figure 5.1 shows a template for an analytic scoring rubric. An analytic rubric has criteria that the teacher (and students) decide are the most important ideas to be mastered in the lesson or task. Below each criterion are listed rankings, or proficiency levels, that will be used to assess how well students master each of the criterion and specific feedback for future learning.

Analytic scoring rubrics provide a separate ranking for each criterion that is being assessed. These amount to a mini-report card at the completion of a product, task, or unit of study. Such ongoing feedback is helpful in increasing the quality of future student work, as it is specific and directly aligned with the task.

Figure 5.2 shows a template for a holistic scoring rubric. A holistic rubric provides a single, overall score for the complete task or product and can be effective when used for a final assessment because of the totality of this kind of rubric. Standards are selected for a high quality product and specific evaluation criteria are chosen for each proficiency level or ranking.

The use of rubrics helps to examine student work in the actual learning process by clearly showing students how their work is being evaluated.

Template for Analytic Scoring Rubrics

Criterion #1

| *Master* | *Expert* | *Apprentice* | *Novice* |

Feedback: _____

_____

Criterion #2

| *Master* | *Expert* | *Apprentice* | *Novice* |

Feedback: _____

_____

Criterion #3

| *Master* | *Expert* | *Apprentice* | *Novice* |

Feedback: _____

_____

Criterion #4

| *Master* | *Expert* | *Apprentice* | *Novice* |

Feedback: _____

_____

FIGURE 5.1   Template for analytic scoring rubric

Rubrics provide a clear teaching directive by helping teachers to clarify exactly what students need to achieve in content and curriculum standards. Rubrics also help students to focus on current and future performance because of the use of specific evaluation criteria. Talika Johnson-Juarez, a third-grade teacher for five years, relates her success with the use of rubrics with her students:

> Rubrics help me to become very clear on exactly what I want my third graders to achieve in both content and performance standards. The process of developing the evaluation criteria for a task makes my instruction clearly related to standards and the way I assess student work. As I select and clarify all critical criteria, ideas for planning and instruction become clearer as well.

Template for a Holistic Scoring Rubric

Proficiency levels or rankings	Descriptions of Criteria
4	Specific evaluation criteria at a "4" level are listed for all selected standards
3	Specific evaluation criteria at a "3" level are listed for all selected standards
2	Specific evaluation criteria at a "2" level are listed for all selected standards
1	Specific evaluation criteria at a "1" level are listed for all selected standards

FIGURE **5.2**   Template for a holistic rubric

At first I created the rubrics with other third-grade teachers in my building. Now I feel confident enough to ask the students to help with selecting the criteria. At the beginning of a lesson or unit I ask my students what qualities they would look for in deciding how to grade the upcoming products. After they come up with five or six criteria, I ask them to rank them according to importance and tell why they ranked them as they did. All of this information is used as the rubric is developed and my students seem to take greater ownership for their work. What a difference this makes in motivation for new lessons and units and in the quality of work. Using rubrics takes the mystery out of evaluation for the students and gives me a feeling of fairness that I don't have with other types of assessment methods.

It is not difficult to see how rubrics can be beneficial to teachers and students alike. Good elementary teachers become even more effective when the direct link between instruction and assessment becomes clarified through the use of rubrics. Rubrics also help teachers to see the connection between the expected success of students and the actual success. Rubrics help students to prepare for a learning experience and increase the chance of success in achievement because students are aware of the specific evaluation criteria before the learning process begins. Using rubrics as they proceed through an authentic learning task encourages the reflective practices of students and helps them set goals and develop ways to reach those goals. Both teachers and students develop a sense of collaboration when using rubrics through clarification and discussion of what quality work is. Rubrics serve, above all, to inform and improve instruction while giving students the feedback they need to learn and grow.

Mr. Washington was right in thinking about the extra benefits in using authentic assessment methods with his students and the cooking station he set up for them. Checklists and product or process rubrics containing evaluation criteria on any of the following would have enhanced student learning:

- mathematics in selection of food quantities
- mathematics in food preparation
- nutritional information
- group process with equity of workload information
- economics issues such as food pricing and budgeting in low-income areas
- life skills such as table setting and manners
- writing invitations to lunch

Student self-assessment would have assisted students in beginning to feel some degree of control over their learning in addition to helping the students and Mr. Washington see progress from one lunch to the next.

The next chapter shows how to design rubrics and how to modify existing rubrics. Several examples of rubrics are given and teachers are encouraged to work in grade-level groups to practice writing their own rubrics.

HELPFUL INTERNET ADDRESSES:

http://www.geocities.com/Athens/Parthenon/8658
An excellent article with many useful links describing ways to implement performance assessments with different populations and in different subject areas

http://www.ncrel.org/sdrs/areas/issues/methods/assment
A group of scholarly reports on various topics related to alternative assessment, providing a good basis for those who wish to explore why one might want to utilize these practices

CHAPTER 6

Designing and Modifying Rubrics

Knowledge comes by taking things apart. But wisdom comes by putting things together.

John A. Morrison

A rubric is defined as an assessment device that uses clearly specified evaluation criteria and proficiency levels that measure student achievement of those criteria. The criteria provide descriptions of each level of performance in terms of what students are able to do. The criteria for a task are known in advance by the students. Products, process, and/or progress may all be evaluated by means of rubrics.

To many teachers, the thought of designing their own rubrics is a daunting task. Once begun, however, the work amounts to systematizing on paper what elementary teachers often attempt to do in their heads: establish evaluation criteria for learning and apply them to individual student work. Heidi Goodrich Andrade (1997) suggests the following steps to consider when beginning to design rubrics:

1. Look at several models. Show students examples of good and not-so-good work. Identify the characteristics that make the good ones good and the bad ones bad.
2. List evaluation criteria. Use the discussion about the models to begin a list of what counts (is essential) in quality work.
3. Articulate gradations of quality for the selected evaluation criteria. Begin by describing the best and worst levels of quality; then fill in the middle levels based on your knowledge of common problems.
4. Practice descriptions of criteria on the models originally observed by having students evaluate the models used in Step 1. Ask students to ask clarification questions and make comments as they evaluate.
5. Use questions and comments to revise rubrics.

When designing and revising rubrics, striving for clear language is a must. Students and teachers must be precise and clear about selected evaluation criteria. A good way to achieve clarity is for the teacher to ask students to interpret what is meant by the evaluation criteria. If student interpretation is correct, then the goal of clarity has been met. If not, student involvement in the selection of more specific or more precise words will help to make the criteria more meaningful and clearer to students. Such involvement empowers the students and, as a result, their learning becomes more focused and self-directed.

There are many rubrics already available to teachers for commonly used authentic assessment tasks. These can be found in staff development workshops, education magazines, and anywhere learner-centered teachers are planning for instruction. The advantages of using rubrics in assessment are that they:

- allow assessment to be more objective
- focus the teacher to clarify criteria in specific terms
- clearly show the students how their work will be evaluated and what is expected
- provide useful feedback regarding the effectiveness of instruction
- provide benchmarks against which to measure progress.

Whether teachers are designing their own rubrics or modifying existing rubrics, the following suggestions will help.

BE SPECIFIC WHEN CHOOSING EVALUATION CRITERIA

Remember that rubrics help to focus on what is expected of students. As the criteria for quality work on a given task are identified, they should be written precisely. Nonspecific, vague words such as creative, interesting, and boring should be avoided because they mean different things to different people. The following examples demonstrate the precision of meaning that specificity adds to a word:

Nonspecific: The opening of the oral presentation was *creative.*
More specific: The presentation opened with an amusing fact, a short demonstration, a colorful visual, or a personal anecdote about the topic.
Nonspecific: The paragraph was *interesting* to the reader.

More specific: Details in the paragraph contain words that are natural, varied, and vivid.

Nonspecific: The presentation was *boring*.

More specific: The presenter spoke in a monotone voice.

More specific criteria help teachers and students alike to hone in on the behaviors that serve to describe great work, mediocre work, or poor work. Focusing on the behaviors and their effect on the product or process will help students to see exactly what they can do to improve their work.

For a relevant example, a common criterion for a visual product is that it shows creativity. As has been shown, the term creativity can have multiple meanings such as exciting, innovative, different, or original. If the task is to design a visual aid, perhaps the fact that it is eye appealing adds specificity to the criterion. The use of specific criteria often enhances teaching as well. Implementing a lesson on what makes a visual aid eye appealing will be more helpful to students than a lesson on what makes a visual aid more creative. The following represents a rubric for a visual presentation using specific criteria, proficiency levels, and a place for specific feedback (see Figure 6.1). It can, of course, be modified to suit the curricular needs of the teacher and students.

All that remains is for the teacher to plan instruction on each of the criteria. For example, lessons on recognizing what is "eye appealing" as well as how to create that effect will increase student success in the task of making a useful visual presentation. Providing models of visual presentations and teaching to the evaluation criteria in the models is a huge step toward enabling students to produce quality work.

INCLUDE SPECIFIC FEEDBACK ON STUDENT WORK

One of the outcomes most commonly noted by teachers who use authentic assessment methods is that it encourages students to take ownership for their learning. The use of specific evaluation criteria is not enough to empower students, however. Students need specific feedback and a chance to reflect on their work and even engage in self-analysis if they are to take charge of their learning. Rubrics can provide us with an efficient means for giving individual student feedback. Such feedback can come from teachers, students, and/or parents depending on the teacher's goals and objectives. The rubric in Figure 6.2 represents an example of the use of teacher feedback on a student's research strategies. Once students have reflected on the feedback, they should be asked to engage in a self-analysis either through a conference, in writing, or both. Conference time for elementary teachers is extremely limited and ways to confer with students efficiently and effectively are discussed in Chapter 9.

Rubric for Visual Presentation

1. The visual presentation is eye appealing.

    Yes   Somewhat   No

Feedback _____

_____

_____

2. The visual presentation presents important information about the question studied.

    Yes   Somewhat   No

Feedback _____

_____

_____

3. The visual presentation can stand alone and be a useful source of information without explanation.

    Yes   Somewhat   No

Feedback _____

_____

_____

4. Artistic strategies, such as the use of different colors and shadings, are used effectively.

    Yes   Somewhat   No

Feedback _____

_____

_____

5. The visual presentation is well organized.

    Yes   Somewhat   No

Feedback _____

_____

_____

FIGURE **6.1** Rubric for visual presentation

Rubric for Research Strategies

1. **The question the student writes and the way it is researched indicates thoughtfulness.**

   Highly demonstrated   Adequately demonstrated   Poorly demonstrated

   Feedback: *The question narrows the subject enough for you to do it justice. You looked up related subjects with ease.*

2. **The student works in a self-disciplined way.**

   Highly demonstrated   Adequately demonstrated   Poorly demonstrated

   Feedback: *You came to me many times for reassurance that you were doing the right thing, although you seemed to know that your approach was correct. You seemed easily distracted by other students when working in the library.*

3. **The student finds different sources of information.**

   Highly demonstrated   Adequately demonstrated   Poorly demonstrated

   Feedback: *Three encyclopedias, one CD-ROM, two books, and an interview made the information comprehensive and interesting.*

4. **The student organizes information and keeps a record of it as it is collected.**

   Highly demonstrated   Adequately demonstrated   Poorly demonstrated

   Feedback: *The notebook you kept with printed copies and notes from readings were very complete.*

5. **The end products reflect in-depth research.**

   Highly demonstrated   Adequately demonstrated   Poorly demonstrated

   Feedback: *Although you had a variety of sources, the written paper reflected just one of those sources. Did you read everything you collected before writing?*

FIGURE **6.2**   Rubric for research strategies

ENCOURAGE STUDENT SELF-ASSESSMENT

Most students desire A grades and yet many, upon earning an A, do not have a clue as to how it happened. This phenomenon is the same for a grade of B, C, D, or F. If pressed, most students will respond that they are either good or bad at something or that the teacher likes or dislikes them. Neither of these explanations involves assessment. Instead, we need to enable students to take ownership for their work through reflection on why their work was either quality work or in need of improvement.

Teachers can give students a chance to assess their own work by asking them to complete the same assessment rubrics that teachers are using. Often, however, these need to be rewritten in terms students can easily understand and using a manner of response easy for them to use. The next example shows a self-assessment rubric for a primary level science journal (see Figure 6.3).

Student self-assessments are useful for reasons beyond helping to empower students. They can give the teacher a glimpse at how students perceive their work. Whether or not the assessments match exactly the assessment of the teacher is not of vital importance. Rather, the teacher's awareness of the student's ability to self-assess accurately may give valuable clues as to how deeply the student understands the tasks as well as how ready the student may be for self-reflection skills. Self-assessments can also provide a starting point for a student-led conference with peers, the teacher, or parents. Giving students a chance to provide feedback on how and why they assessed their work as they did helps the teacher guide them toward realistic goals for improvement.

USE ANY FORMAT YOU LIKE

Elementary teachers have their own organizational schema which help them to take in information in an easily comprehended form. Rubric formats can be made to fit any schema. The only things we need to keep in mind is that

---

Science Journal on Plants

Student Self-Assessment

Directions: Put a sticker above the words that best tell about your work.

Did you write in your journal at least twice a week?	I did.	Sometimes I did.	Not at all.
Did you illustrate each entry?	I did.	Sometimes I did.	Not at all.
Did you share your observation with at least one other person?	I did.	Sometimes I did.	I did not.
Did you use correct punctuation and capital letters in each entry?	I did.	Sometimes I did.	Need help.

FIGURE **6.3**   Student self-assessment for plant journal

the form should contain specific evaluation criteria, levels of proficiency, and some method of giving specific feedback. To illustrate this point, the following rubrics are formatted in two different ways; yet both address group process.

The first rubric (see Figure 6.4) separates the criteria and scores each criterion separately. This form may be most helpful when the teacher determines that the criteria are still relatively new to students and would like students to focus on the individual criteria.

The second form for the same topic presents a more holistic look at group process (see Figure 6.5). Teachers may wish to change the formatting of rubrics that are used often in order to maintain student interest. It is important to note that holistic scoring does not analyze the strengths or weaknesses of each part of the task separately. Teachers may wish to use such a rubric as students develop fluency in the processes being evaluated.

The ranking words used to define proficiency levels can be developed with the students to provide variety from always using grades, numbers, or the same ranking worlds for every rubric. For example, a rubric that assesses student work on a mural might have the following ranking words:

Master   Veteran   Apprentice   Novice

For a social studies project on Egypt, the following words might be useful:

Pharaoh   Noble   Artisan   Peasant

It is important to remember that these are not meant to be overall ratings for the child's work, but are used to evaluate students' performance of each of the criteria in the rubric. Selecting ranking words could prove to be an enjoyable activity for students and help them to appreciate the effort to choose words that are not negatively judgmental.

It is important to remember that developing rubrics is a cooperative task and that, during the learning stage, teachers need release time in order to meet by grade levels to plan authentic tasks and select the evaluation criteria that they will be using. As teachers create or modify rubrics, it is important to select specific evaluation criteria, include specific feedback on student work, provide a means for student self-assessment, and use any format that is clear and easy to read for both the teacher and the students.

The next chapter will focus on rubrics for processes and products and ways to measure progress for both process and product outcomes. The role of self-assessment and ways to encourage self-assessment will also be discussed.

Rubric for Group Process

Group Process	Excellent	Satisfactory	Needs Improvement
Level of participation	Each member was equally involved in the process.	Most members were active in the process.	One or two members dominated discussion and led the process.
Cooperative Effort	There was evidence that each member contributed to the final product.	Most members contributed to the final product.	One or two members completed the final product.
Listening	Members made eye contact with the speaker. Body movement kept to a minimum by all.	Most members attended to the speaker.	Members did not attend to the speaker and seemed intent on speaking over others.
On-task behavior	Discussion was on the topic with no distractions noted.	Some off-task behavior was noted, but group members got one another right back on task.	Much off-task discussion occurred. Group had to be brought back on task by others.
Interactions	Words of politeness noted. Very few interruptions.	Polite words were often used. Some interruptions and impulsive behavior noted.	Group members behaved impulsively; polite words were not in evidence.

Feedback _____

_____

_____

_____

_____

FIGURE 6.4   Group process rubric

Rubric for Group Process

Rating	Description
Excellent	The level of participation was strong. Each member was equally involved in the process. Cooperative effort was superior with each member contributing to the group effort. Members listened and made eye contact with the speaker and kept body movement to a minimum. Discussion was on the topic with no distractions noted. The interactions are positive with words of politeness noted and very few interruptions of group members.
Satisfactory	Most members participated in the process. Cooperative effort was good with most members contributing to the final product. Most members attended to the speaker. Some off-task behavior was noted, but group members got one another right back on task. Interactions were good. Polite words were often used. Some interruptions and impulsive behavior noted.
Needs Improvement	One or two members dominated discussion and led the process. One or two members completed the final product. Members did not attend to the speaker and seemed intent on speaking over one another. Much off-task discussion occurred. The group had to be brought back on task by others. Polite words were not in evidence. Group members behaved impulsively.

Feedback _____

_____

_____

FIGURE **6.5**   Holistic group process rubric

HELPFUL INTERNET ADDRESSES:

http://www.school.discovery.com/schrockguide/assess.html
Kathy Schrock's Guide for Educators offering subject-specific and general rubrics for teacher use

http://www.interactiveclassroom.com
Includes techniques for creating rubrics, standards for criteria assessment and strategies for negotiable contracting

CHAPTER 7

Measuring Products, Process, Progress, and Student Self-Assessment

To conform to the widespread concern that all that is taught be measured, teachers . . . are required to stuff students with fragments of measurable knowledge as if the students had no needs—almost as if they were things. Education is defined as how many fragments of information these "student-things" can retain long enough to be measured on standardized achievement tests. Most competent teachers recognize, however, that this approach has little or nothing to do with what they consider quality education.

William Glasser in The Quality School

In elementary classrooms of today, teachers plan beneficial lessons that integrate subject matter and present students with authentic tasks that mirror those in real life. Such complexity of instruction requires an equally complex assessment system. This chapter presents rubric examples for typical elementary school products, process, and progress in addition to rubrics for student self-assessment. These areas of assessment help to complete the assessment paradigm for teachers and students (see Figure 7.1).

According to this paradigm, teachers plan integrated instruction and students complete work that includes the use of processes, the gathering of information, and the creation of products. Students are then asked to examine their work by completing a self-assessment which, along with the teacher's evaluation of student work, leads to an awareness of progress and the setting of new goals by the student with the teacher's help. The self-assessment and goal-setting part of this assessment paradigm helps to foster a collaborative effort between students and teachers in the teaching/learning process. In a collaborative environment, students can begin to take charge of their learning through self-assessment and goal setting. Assessment is seen as evaluating

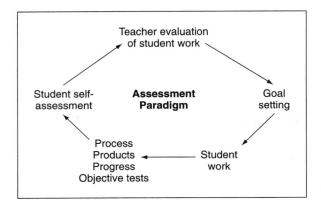

FIGURE 7.1   Assessment paradigm for integrated instruction

whether one has learned what one intended to learn, the effectiveness of learning strategies, the quality of products and decisions about which products reflect one's best work, the usefulness of the materials used in a task, and whether remediation is needed and how that remediation might be realized. Understanding how to assess products, process, and progress helps elementary teachers to see the connections between instruction and assessment.

QUALITY PRODUCTS

Products are the concrete outcomes of student effort and often contain factual knowledge-level content. While the knowledge acquisition part of learning can be measured by objective-type tests, the product also asks students to use the knowledge in some real-world way. Students can create products alone or in groups and seem to enjoy "project work" where many of these products are developed. When planning project work within an integrated unit of study, the best elementary teachers give students choices of product outcomes. These choices help students to choose products that reflect their style of learning and interests.

The following list represents a sampling of authentic products often completed by elementary students.

- posters
- research paper
- model
- written story

- cookbook
- video
- oral presentation
- storytelling
- speech
- lab report
- song
- journal entry

This list can go on and on and is only limited by the imagination of the students and teacher. Teachers who brainstorm possible product outcomes with students increase the chance that students will take ownership in their learning. For example, a primary teacher taught lessons on how to care for a pet, which animals make good pets, and people in real life who care for pets as part of their job. As part of the assessment piece, students were asked to create a product entitled "A Day in the Life of a Pet". The teacher's objectives were to enhance student observational skills and check on the accuracy of student understanding of appropriate pet care. Students who did not have a pet could work with someone who did or adopt any one of the classroom pets available as part of the unit. When given a choice of product, some students wrote and illustrated a story, some produced a video, and others gave an oral presentation using the pet as a live visual aid. Having the product rubrics on hand for each product enabled the teacher to efficiently teach to the critical attributes of a good product right at the beginning of the assignment.

Many elementary teachers will say that, before the use of rubrics, product work was often mediocre at best. Students gave oral presentations, handed in posters and collages, and built models without the benefit of clear evaluation criteria. Consequently, most teachers admit that they didn't really assess the products but counted them as part of "enrichment" or "extra credit". The following rubrics (see Figures 7.2, 7.3, and 7.4) show how the evaluation criteria for three products can help students to produce quality work and help teachers to fairly assess the work.

Once the evaluation criteria are established, the teacher must present models of posters where the criteria are highly demonstrated. Next, the teacher should teach students how to successfully satisfy the specific criteria. For example, students should be taught how to gather accurate information and pare it down so that only the salient points are included in the poster. How to present information pictorially or graphically so that it is "eye-catching" would also be demonstrated. The inclusion of the criteria helps the teacher to plan instruction and, in the spirit of collaboration, part of the planning would probably include the art teacher as well.

Poster Production

Criteria	1	2	3
Accurate information is presented	Highly demonstrated	Adequately demonstrated	Poorly demonstrated
Information is easily understood	Highly demonstrated	Adequately demonstrated	Poorly demonstrated
Information is shown in an eye-catching manner	Highly demonstrated	Adequately demonstrated	Poorly demonstrated
Correct mechanics are used (spelling, usage, grammar)	Highly demonstrated	Adequately demonstrated	Poorly demonstrated

Specific feedback and comments:

FIGURE 7.2 Rubric for assessment of poster

This rubric for a model is a generic one and can be used with a great deal of the elementary school curricula. A unit on "Simple Machines" or "Butterflies", for example, would present many opportunities for building models. As explained in Chapter 6, modifying the rubric to suit instruction can be done at the discretion of the teacher. For example, the kinds of materials to be used or the size and scale of the model may be desirable evaluation criteria a teacher would want to include the rubric.

The next example (see Figure 7.4) addresses a group product in the form of an oral presentation. As previously mentioned, individual assessment of content can be evaluated in additional ways. Perhaps the teacher would give each student an objective test or an essay to determine the amount of information acquired by individual students. For the group presentation, the teacher, prior to the task, explains the means by which quality work is produced. There would be lessons on gathering content information, the appropriate use of audiovisual materials, the roles of individuals in the group, and the desired effect of the presentation on the audience.

Group rubrics tend to contain evaluation criteria for group process, since the efforts of individual group members help to determine the success of the product. As good teachers know, teaching the process of learning is an ongoing task for all elementary teachers.

Making Models

1. The model is neat in appearance.

   excellent   good   limited   poor

Feedback: _____

_____

2. The model is an accurate representation of what you are studying.

   excellent   good   limited   poor

Feedback: _____

_____

3. The model is well constructed.

   excellent   good   limited   poor

Feedback: _____

_____

4. Artistic strategies such as choice, variety, and use of materials are used effectively.

   excellent   good   limited   poor

Feedback: _____

_____

FIGURE 7.3   Assessment rubric for a model

PROCESS

The process of learning is a series of actions and behavior that lead toward a desired result such as clear communication or effective teamwork. Process includes all strategies, decisions, rough drafts, and rehearsals used in completing a task. The process of writing, for example, includes brainstorming for relevant ideas, organizing an outline or web of ideas, creating rough drafts, and using editing feedback on the final piece. Teamwork in group or project tasks uses the process skills of leadership, decision making, communication, and conflict management. The process of both individual and group tasks mirror the process expected in real life. Knowing how to work toward common goals is an important component in all life skills, including the world of work.

Group Oral Presentation

Levels	Content	Audiovisual	Individuals	Audience
Excellent	Accurate, specific, research-based, retold in own words	Unique, adds to presentation quality of materials used, neatness, clear message	Each member is equally involved in presentation and is well-informed about the topic	Maintains eye contact with presenters, totally involved, asks many questions
Good	Less detailed, lacking depth, limited number of sources used	Material supports topic, but does not enhance presentation; some attempts at originality, clear message	Most members are active; most are informed about the topic	Some of audience not attending; questions are limited or off-target
Minimal	Limited information, general, strays from topic, not presented in own words	Inappropriate materials, no originality, detracts from presentation; message is confusing	One or two members dominate; some members do not seem well prepared or well informed	Audience is not attending; no questions asked or questions are off the topic

Specific feedback and comments: _____

_____

_____

_____

FIGURE **7.4**   Rubric for oral presentation by a group

Skills for an effective process must be taught to students just as purposefully as academic skills. For decades elementary teachers struggled with assigning an "effort" grade to student report cards and did so intuitively. In large part, teachers simply directed students to engage in teamwork or to do their best work and that directive was not enough. Students need to know *how* one behaves as a teammate and *how* to achieve their best work. Rubrics on the process of learning help students to hone in on the specific criteria needed to acquire effective process skills.

The process of listening is a behavior that all students need in order to succeed in individual and group work. Additionally, listening, speaking, reading, and writing are components of every elementary language arts program. A teacher can use the rubric in Figure 7.5 to score a student's listening performance as observed by the teacher while the student is engaged in work with others. As with all rubrics, process rubrics can be modified to suit the scenario for intended use. Whatever the criteria used by the teacher, models for the criteria that earn a top score need to be presented by the teacher. Once the teacher models and teaches to high standards for listening and the students' attempts at listening are assessed, the chances increase that students will become more proficient at listening.

The rubric in Figure 7.6 is intended for use with any group process, including cooperative learning. The creator of this rubric sees the behavior of individuals in the group as a key to moving the group forward to successful

Listening Rubric

Score	Evaluation Criteria
4 Excellent	Listens attentively, maintains eye contact with speaker.
	Recalls information accurately.
	Asks relevant questions to seek understanding.
	Makes relevant comments during discussion.
	Takes turns, accepts other opinions and ideas.
3 Good	Listens attentively, maintains eye contact some of the time.
	Recalls most information.
	Asks questions, but they're not always relevant.
	Sometimes uses opinions of others, but doesn't always let them finish speaking.
2 Poor	Inattentive, easily distracted, fidgety.
	Limited recall of information.
	Makes irrelevant comments and asks no questions.
	Interrupts while others are speaking.
0 Failure	No attempt to listen.

FIGURE **7.5** Scoring rubric for listening

Rubric for Teamwork Behavior

Behavior	Evaluation Criteria		
	Excellent	**Good**	**Needs Improvement**
Involvement	Each member is equally involved in the process and contributes to the task.	Most members are active in the process and contribute to the task.	One or two members dominate discussion and influence the process.
Listening	All members attend to whoever is speaking.	Most members attend to the speaker.	Members are not attending to one another.
Staying on track	Discussion is on topic with no distractions noted.	Some off-task behavior is noted, but group members get one another right back on task.	Much off-task discussion occurs. Group has to be brought back on task by others.
Conduct	Members use polite speech. No interruptions are noted.	Polite words are often used. Some interrupting and impulsive behavior.	Members behave impulsively. Polite speech is not in evidence.

Feedback: _____

_____

_____

FIGURE 7.6   Scoring rubric for teamwork behaviors

task completion. This teacher would describe an excellent group process as one in which group members were equally involved in the process, attended to one another without distractibility, and used methods of communication that encouraged useful problem-solving behaviors.

Rubrics that emphasize group process skills make students aware of the processes that help to advance the group toward a common goal—completion of the task. As students practice using interpersonal skills and contribute to group maintenance by effectively performing a variety of roles, they learn valuable life skills transferable to many learning situations.

STUDENT SELF-ASSESSMENT AND EVALUATING PROGRESS

Self-reflection plays an important role in authentic assessment because reflection helps students develop the ability to consider the worth of their own work against publicly stated standards. Through this ability to self-assess, students can revise and modify their work to successfully meet the standards. Initially it will be difficult for students to make self-assessments on the quality of their own work because schools so rarely ask students to do so. When students are first introduced to self-assessment, good teachers model the process of reflection and demonstrate the benefits of assessing one's own work. Praising the effort that goes into work and appreciating the amount of thinking that takes place when completing a task help students to view reflection and self-assessment as desirable behaviors. The pride and self-satisfaction in analyzing one's own work and making appropriate modifications is empowering to students.

Recognizing progress that is being made is equally empowering. As students become self-directed in their work, they realize that the key to progress is in meeting the evaluation criteria for a product or process. Using the criteria to compare identical work samples over time helps students to reflect on their level of progress. Students begin to know what strengths are reflected in their work and how to make goals for improvement in future work. Chapter 8 discusses the use of portfolios as a vehicle for assisting teachers and students to assess progress.

Self-assessment procedures for products, process, and progress can be applied to individual or group work. The key to self-assessment is to focus on the evaluation criteria and the student's reflection on the degree to which the criteria were met. Reflection questions designed for assessing the group process in Figure 7.6, the Rubric for Teamwork Behavior, might look like this:

1. Was your group successful at achieving its goals? Why?
2. What roles did group members play?
3. What did your group find most challenging?
4. Describe any problems you encountered.
5. Explain how one person helped the group through a tough time or decision.
6. What evidence can you give that shows how successfully your group contributed to this activity.

After receiving individual responses to these questions, the teacher can meet with the group to discuss the results. Individual perceptions of the group process can be enlightening to other group members and cause continued reflection. For example, one student may have defined playing a leadership role as one who makes as many decisions as possible. Another person may have seen this person not as a leader, but rather as someone who had difficulty considering the ideas of others. After a thoughtful deliberation of all the responses, the teacher can then facilitate group goal-setting for future work. Of course, such conferences are most productive in collaborative classrooms with supportive teachers and students.

Ongoing individual assessment also helps students to reflect on existing strengths in their work and to make specific suggestions on how goals for improvement will be implemented. Figure 7.7 shows a self-reflection form for a retelling by writing task completed by a primary-level student.

Retelling (by writing and illustrating)

Directions: Think about your work. Read the question to yourself while I read it out loud. Circle the answer that best tells about your work.

1. Does my retelling have at least three facts?

Yes   No

2. Are the facts correct?

Yes   No   Some of them are.

3. Does my picture go with the retelling?

Yes   No   Part of it does.

4. Do my sentences begin with capital letters?

All of the time   Some of the time.   Never

5. Do my sentences end correctly with a period, question mark, or exclamation point?

Yes   No

6. Did I use other resources to check my spelling?

Yes   No

FIGURE 7.7   Self-assessment form for a retelling assignment

After students complete the self-reflection form, they are given a chance to use their reflective responses to make any necessary modifications before handing their work to the teacher for evaluation purposes. With the second retelling by writing and illustrating assignment, students can look at their progress by comparing the first self-reflection form with the second one. The form in Figure 7.8 will assist young learners with looking at their progress in the identical task of retelling by writing and illustrating.

Conferring with the teacher on the responses from individual self-reflection will help the student with the accuracy of continued self-reflection as the teacher encourages the student to provide evidence for responses. This is especially important for the young learner and all beginners of self-assessment. In addition, students will need help with specific suggestions on how to do better on future work. For example, if a student says that spelling is an area of improvement for the next written retelling, a means of implementing actual improvement may include the keeping of a word log as one is reading the story for the first time. The student can write down a word in the log that might be used in the written retelling. The student then has an active plan for improving spelling in the next identical or similar task.

My Writing Progress

Directions: Look at your first retelling and your second retelling. Think about the things you have gotten better at doing.

1. Underline all the things that you have gotten better in doing.

   writing correct facts
   using capital letters and end marks properly
   making a picture that goes with the story
   checking my spelling

2. I am really proud of _____

   _____

   _____

3. Things I want to do better on my next retelling are _____

   _____

FIGURE **7.8**   Self-reflection form for progress on retelling

The assessment of products, process, and progress is not an easy one. Teachers need to have regular grade-level meeting times established where appropriate rubrics and self-assessment forms can be designed collaboratively. In the opening quote, William Glasser suggested that most competent teachers recognize that information measurement has little to do with what they consider quality education to be. It is absolutely necessary for school districts to provide teachers with the time needed to develop the kinds of tasks and assessment measures that address products, process, and progress. As teachers work together to create new assessments, their students benefit from a more complete assessment of their work. The next chapter looks at the use of portfolios in elementary classrooms.

HELPFUL INTERNET ADDRESSES:

http://www.sccoe.k12.ca.us/stcregion5/student
This site looks at the rationale behind and the outcomes of student self-assessment

http://www.idea.uml.edu/assessment/higgins2a.html
Includes several concrete alternative assessment activities for the primary grades

CHAPTER 8

Portfolios: Purposes and Contents

"Here's my portfolio. I did all this work by myself. I like this (holding up a report) the best because I am proud that I could do all that writing. I used the computer and fixed stuff until it looked like this. I did all this myself. Jason is my peer partner and he gave me some good suggestions, but I made all the changes myself. Look at my greenhouse model. Wanna know how it works? I made it all by myself. See the beads of water? That's condensation. Know what that is? I do. I can make it happen and I wrote a whole paragraph on it. All by myself. What do you want to look at first?"

Talisha, age 8
In "conversation" with Janitor Bob
At a classroom portfolio party

There is hardly an elementary teacher in the entire country who does not know the value of keeping a work sample folder for students throughout the year. Students like to look at their progress in concrete terms and parents enjoy looking at their child's work at conference time. Work folders also help the teacher to provide documentation and evidence for report card grades and teacher comments. Because of this widespread practice of collecting student work, elementary teachers are receptive to learning more about what portfolios are and the benefits derived from portfolio use.

Portfolio assessment demands authenticity because the making of a portfolio mirrors real-world circumstances. Artists, writers, journalists, actors, musicians, architects, and anyone else who engages in active, performance-based work benefits from compiling a portfolio of their work. A photographer interviewing for a wedding shoot brings along a portfolio of wedding photographs to show the quality of work one can expect. A journalist has writing samples that demonstrate the depth and breadth of his or her work, musicians keep audio and videotapes to compare their performances, and architects have sample drawings of buildings they have designed as well as buildings they would like to see built. Each of these collections of work, or portfolios, is representative of the ability and achievement of the person who created the work.

Portfolios have a self-evaluation component where students are expected to take ownership for assessing their own learning. Each piece of work in the portfolios mentioned above was selected with pre-established criteria in mind—mostly criteria that look at best work. Prospective clients or employers make judgments about the quality of work in the portfolio as part of the hiring process. While elementary teachers are not "hiring" students, the evaluative nature of the portfolio appeals to teachers who are mentoring students and regularly evaluating student progress toward best work. Good teachers are concerned that their students are learning through the performance of worthwhile tasks and that their students are empowered through self-assessment.

In elementary schools portfolios are, simply put, a purposeful collection of student work that exhibits the student's products, processes, and progress in one or more areas. The portfolios may include students' best work or benchmark samples that show student progress over time in a variety of areas. According to Martin-Kniep (1997), there are significant ways in which portfolios differ from work sample folders:

1. the portfolio must include student participation in selecting contents;
2. criteria for selecting work for inclusion into the portfolio must be present;
3. criteria for judging the merit of work must also be present; and
4. there should be some evidence of student reflection present in the portfolio.

The value of having criteria for the contents and assessment of a portfolio is the same as having criteria for rubrics. Students can focus on the process of learning and be able to make modifications to their work before submitting a final product.

Adding the conditions of collaborative selection of portfolio contents and student self-reflection fosters the use of metacognitive strategies recommended by cognitive development researchers. There is much agreement in cognitive research that suggests that it is extremely important to create situations in which students must think about their own thinking—reflect on the ways in which they learn and why they fail to learn (Flavell, 1979; Flower, 1986; & Sternberg, 1986). As a result of such self-reflection, students revise and modify their work and take the initiative to assess their own progress. A major goal of authentic assessment is to help students develop the capacity to evaluate their own work against public standards (Darling-Hammond, Ancess, & Falk, 1995), in this case the criteria for judging the merit of the work that goes into the portfolio. The process and criteria for portfolio development allows students to engage in the very important process of self-assessment.

Kirsten Rochelle, an elementary teacher in the Spencer-VanEtten School District in upstate New York, reflects on the effects of establishing a portfolio system for herself and her students:

> As I look at it now, portfolio assessment incorporates and pulls together several of those areas of overall assessment that I wanted to focus on more deeply, such as conferencing, self-assessment and reflection, reporting to parents, and providing students with more ownership for their learning. I now see portfolios as a logical and important piece of my classroom.
>
> The more I read and discuss with others, the more it seems to me that portfolios are a natural part of a student-centered classroom. By using portfolios, students take on greater responsibility and ownership for their learning. Portfolios can be used as a means for a student to see personal growth, reflect on learning, and show best work. A portfolio can also provide opportunities for students to make choices and sharpen decision-making skills. Portfolios can take the development of interdisciplinary connections a step further as students create portfolios with a theme. This kind of assessment can provide a much clearer picture of a student's work than the conventional graded system can.

Clearly, Kirsten sees the numerous benefits of portfolio assessment in her collaborative, student-centered classroom environment. Using teacher observation skills, conferring with students and parents, and negotiating the contents of the written, oral, and visual work that goes into the portfolio all increase the chance that students will take responsibility for the process of learning.

KINDS AND PURPOSES OF PORTFOLIOS

There are many books and articles on the types of portfolios for classroom use. Even though the names for the kinds of portfolios differ, there are three main examples most often mentioned. These examples each have a clear-cut purpose:

- **Product Portfolios:** *Portfolios that contain products that are judged to be the students' best work.* These are often called Display Portfolios, Showcase Portfolios, Best Work Portfolios, or Achievement Portfolios. For example, sample contents might include a videotape of a performance, a model, a piece of writing, or artwork

- **Process Portfolios:** *Portfolios that contain work that provides evidence of how works evolved and were refined.* These are sometimes called Effort Portfolios. Contents of this kind of portfolio might include all drafts leading to a completed product or a paragraph describing the roles a student played in order to move group work toward a common goal.
- **Progress Portfolios:** *Portfolios that compare identical work samples over time in order to show student improvement or growth over time.* These are sometimes called Work in Progress or the Working Portfolio. This portfolio contains work completed as first and last parallel assignments in either or both process and product tasks.

As stated previously, each kind of portfolio will have evidence of student self-assessment as well as contents related to the portfolio's purpose. In addition, many teachers see a need to establish portfolios with a combination of purposes. For example, students who have developed proficiency in assembling portfolios can be asked to assess both process and products of a unit of study. Likewise, students who would benefit from a holistic look at how their work is progressing might be asked to assess progress by looking at first and last parallel process *and* product tasks. It is important to keep in mind that teachers who are skilled in portfolio use recommend starting slowly. Choosing a single purpose helps everyone involved to become very familiar with the process of assembling and assessing a portfolio before establishing more complex purposes.

CONTENTS OF PORTFOLIOS

After the purpose of the portfolio is established, teachers and students can begin to negotiate contents. The variety of content selection is only limited by the degree of inventive thinking by teachers as they plan for instruction. Because the authentic possibilities for selection of content are vast, it is recommended that teachers have a collaborative planning time for sharing possible entries for inclusion in portfolios. The following represents a partial list of possible entries and should be added to as teachers and students think of additional suggestions:

- computer disks
- journal entries
- letters
- interest inventories
- inventions

- reading lists
- maps
- poetry
- murals
- essays/reports
- photographs
- designs
- posters
- science log entries
- models
- art work
- videotapes
- lab experiment reports
- solutions to problems
- quizzes and tests

The contents of the portfolio are determined, in large part, by the interdisciplinary theme selected for a unit of study. Such themes are suggested in state curriculum guides because they address the learning standards that the states expect teachers to meet. Once the theme is selected, elementary teachers begin to intertwine and integrate all applicable content area objectives for a particular grade level into lessons, exercises, and authentic tasks. The following description of portfolio assessment in an integrated, thematic unit plan illustrates what a portfolio might look like.

PORTFOLIOS IN PRACTICE

Katie Goyette, a teacher from Holy Family Primary School in Elmira, New York, planned a unit on tropical rain forests for intermediate level students. Ms. Goyette felt that the study of the rain forest ecosystem would help students to investigate the deterioration and destruction of the rain forests with the goal of helping students to understand that actions in one part of the world affect other parts of the world. Also, students would be encouraged to engage in critical thinking and problem solving as they determined ways in which the rain forests could be preserved. Several authentic tasks were planned so the unit would last for three weeks.

Ms. Goyette designed a portfolio assessment that had the purpose of showing best work. Students were advised that, upon completion of the unit, there would be a portfolio party. Each student could invite one person such

---

Best Work Evaluation Form

Student Name _____

Title of Task _____

Directions: Please write your answers to questions in complete, well-written sentences.

1. What about this piece makes it your best work?
2. What new thing(s) did you learn from doing this task?
3. What would you change about the task or your final product if you were to do this task again?
4. What advice would you give to future students who were about to complete this task?

FIGURE **8.1**   Best work evaluation form

as a family member, a student from another room, a teacher, a lunch aide, the janitor or a neighbor, for example. The twofold purpose of the party was to be able to explain to someone else what students had learned and to educate their guest on the issues surrounding the rain forest ecosystem. Students were instructed to choose five products from the rain forest unit that they felt to be their finest work. To assist students in reflecting on the quality of their work, Ms. Goyette asked students to complete an evaluation form for each selection they chose to include in their portfolio (see Figure 8.1).

The evaluation form gives the students a structure from which to engage in reflection. It provides the students with focus questions, or prompts, that help students to think deeply about their work. Such prompts are key to assisting the student in identifying quality work. Furthermore the teacher not only gains useful information about the student's learning, but also gains important feedback on the task itself.

Ms. Goyette also asked students to create a table of contents page for their portfolio (see Figure 8.2). The completed portfolios would be the focal point of discussion at the portfolio party, complete with refreshments from the rain forest regions. As the students inform their guests about the rain forest, the guests cannot help but see the benefits of authentic learning tasks that are organized around a central theme and that are relevant and beneficial to students.

Within such integrated instruction, students use knowledge from a variety of disciplines. The stress is on the use of knowledge and how students

Table of Contents

Rain Forest Unit Work by Jessica

Entry	Page
A. Photograph of greenhouse model	1
Chart of temperature readings	
Best Work Evaluation Form	
B. Paper on "The Destruction of the Rain forests and How We Can Save Them"	4
Peer conference notes	
Best Work Evaluation Form	
C. Tropical rain forests of the world map	8
Paragraph on why I think the rain forests are located on or near the equator	
Best Work Evaluation Form	
D. Brochure for a rain forest tour	11
Brochure rubric completed by me	
Best Work Evaluation Form	
E. Photograph of rain forest awareness poster	14
Poster rubric completed by me	
Best Work Evaluation Form	

FIGURE 8.2   Sample Table of Contents

learn. Teachers can assess separate learning components as they wish. For example, Ms. Goyette could ask her students to write a letter to a local newspaper editor about solving the problems of the disappearing rain forest. She can then separately evaluate the level of communication skills, interpersonal skills, and science understanding that students have. Some of this evaluation can be made with the use of rubrics and some with objective style tests. It is up to the teacher to decide upon whatever evaluation methods are best aligned with the teacher's instruction and the state standards.

The assessment of the learning that has taken place within an integrated thematic unit is aided by the use of a portfolio. The students benefit from organizing and reflecting on their work and the teacher knows how the students are thinking about their work. Teachers who plan this way determine during the planning process what the essential learning is and how it will be evaluated. An important thing to remember is that in authentic assessment, knowledge and skills are essential and inseparable; content knowledge becomes a means to an end, not the end in itself (Hart, 1994).

VARIATIONS FOR YOUNG CHILDREN

The purpose, contents, and use of the portfolio are the same for young children as they are for more accomplished readers and writers. The early childhood teacher makes use of more checklists to accompany work samples given over time. Students and parents can note progress made from unit to unit by observing the increased number of skills that are mastered from a beginning piece of work to a later selection. For example, a young child may move from drawing pictures with a few descriptive words scrawled beneath to a three-sentence "story" using inventive spelling. Audio tapes can reveal progress made in oral reading and video tapes can record a variety of performances.

Electronic portfolios can also be useful with young children. Michael Simons, a kindergarten teacher in Ithaca, New York, scans student products throughout work on integrated, thematic units and students use a simple drawing program to present their ideas and thoughts pictorially. Students who are at a pre-writing stage can record their story to accompany their drawings while others can use word processing programs. Parents are encouraged at all times to come to school to view these electronic portfolios. In addition to unit work, Mr. Simons has a total school portfolio with work samples from all content areas. Work samples are collected in September, January, and May and a disk goes home three times a year with every child. Parents can also view the disk at school with their child at regularly scheduled conference time. Electronic portfolios can be easily used with older children as well.

MANAGING PORTFOLIOS

Teachers have many questions about the management of portfolios in the classroom and there are no single correct responses to such questions. Rather, teachers should consider the answers to the following typical questions in light of their particular school community and the characteristics of their school population:

> **Q:** How long should a portfolio last? Some school personnel say that portfolios should be kept for a year and passed on to the next year's teacher. This seems a bit daunting.
>
> **A:** It has been the contention in this book that the methods of authentic assessment, including the portfolio, be used by teachers and their students for regular, ongoing classroom instruction. Statewide assessment or even schoolwide assessment needs differ in that they wish to look at more long-term data, perhaps for a year or more. While there is much literature that addresses this issue, such is not the purpose

of this book. The length of portfolio use for classroom assessment is actually determined by the scope of the teacher's planning. Typically, portfolios can provide classroom assessment opportunities for primary students at the end of a few weeks of study and intermediate students for longer periods of up to six weeks or so.

Q: What kinds of containers do teachers use for holding the contents of the portfolio?

A: Portfolios in elementary schools can contain journals, project work, video tapes of performance, as well as student work samples, rubrics, checklists, and self-assessments to name some of the possibilities. This can seem difficult to collect and store. It is suggested that students have access to a camera for capturing photographs of large, cumbersome objects such as sculpture, models, murals, and the like. Some containers for portfolios include:

- folders of all kinds
- three-ring binders
- scrapbooks and photo albums
- shoeboxes (all the same size for easy storage)
- vertical "cubbies" with pull-out plastic bins
- pizza boxes
- computer disks

Whichever container is selected for use, it is important to keep in mind that the portfolio should be easily accessible to both students and teachers.

Q: Should portfolios go home? What if students don't bring them back to school?

A: Portfolios should definitely go home. After the goal-setting conference and the teacher's final assessment is made, there is no reason why the portfolio shouldn't remain at home if that is what the student wishes. Parents, of course, will have received a description of the unit at the beginning of the unit so that they can be given an opportunity to contribute to the learning in any way they choose. With full knowledge of the unit objectives, it is fair to assume that final completion of the unit and the portfolio would be eagerly awaited by many families.

Q: Should portfolios be saved and sent on to the students' new teacher at the start of a new school year?

A: Many teachers say that portfolios should not be sent to the next year's teacher and the reasons for this decision are as follows:

- The problem of storing thirty portfolios per classroom over the summer is one of monumental proportions in many elementary schools.

Most schools simply do not have the space it would take to stack thirty pizza boxes or thirty shoeboxes.

- Students like to take their work home to share with others. This sharing is an important process in enhancing the intrinsic "good feelings" that are connected with learning.

- Many teachers do not see the value of going through nearly thirty three-month-old portfolios at the start of a new school year. Instead, teachers would like to invite all students to share their successes with others in any way they wish. This provides the student with a way to convey current successes to teachers and students in a new classroom situation.

Administrators, faculty, and staff should discuss all questions surrounding the management of portfolios in order to find the solutions that are right for their particular physical plant and school population. The problems become less significant when portfolios are sent home after the completion of a unit. For year-long comparisons of work samples, computer disks are probably the best answer to the storage problems.

It is worth the effort to ask and find solutions to the questions teachers have about portfolio assessment so that learners like Talisha, at the beginning of this chapter, will develop enthusiasm for their work and start on the road to lifelong learning. The next chapter will examine the methods of self-assessment and present goal-setting opportunities for students and teachers.

HELPFUL INTERNET ADDRESS:

http://www.ericae.net/intboda.htm#AA
ERIC Clearinghouse on Assessment and Evaluation:
Alternative/Performance-Based Assessment

CHAPTER 9

Self-Assessment and Goal-Setting Opportunities

Children should be led to make their own investigations and to draw their own inferences. They should be told as little as possible and induced to discover as much as possible. Self-evolution guarantees a vividness and permanency of impression which the usual methods can never produce. Any piece of knowledge which the pupil himself solved becomes by virtue of the conquest much more thoroughly his than it could else be.

James L. Hughes
In Mistakes in Teaching
Published in 1893

The ability to self-reflect, accept and use feedback, and set realistic goals for oneself is, in today's world and in the world of James Hughes over one hundred years ago, essential to working relationships in any job or career. Knowing some information as a result of schooling is not enough; knowing *how* to become informed is the means to opening doors to any area one wishes to explore. Such is the goal of every good elementary teacher—to teach students to become proficient at how they learn best. The use of authentic assessment methods helps teachers and students to realize that goal. Portfolios, in particular, provide students with a vehicle for communicating to themselves and others how they plan, oversee, and assess their own learning. According to O'Malley and Pierce (1996), a portfolio is a unique opportunity for students to learn to monitor their own progress and take responsibility for meeting goals set jointly with the teacher. No matter what the purpose of the portfolio is, students are always asked to assess, or evaluate, the quality of their work whether it be product or process work. The use of pre-established criteria, or standards, for quality work and the use of specific feedback help students set specific goals for improvement in future work. This cycle of self-assessment—feedback and goal setting—provides the means for students to become empowered with monitoring their own learning.

SELF-ASSESSMENT

Student self-assessment is at the heart of the assessment reform movement where students are asked to take the initiative to evaluate their own progress (Tierney, Carter, & Desai, 1991). In their work with almost a hundred school districts around the United States that are engaged in science education reform, Hein and Price (1994) found that:

> Student self-evaluations can be included in the assessment process. They provide unique information to teachers and also encourage self-reflection. Although students may occasionally rate themselves unrealistically high, teachers report that this is not usually the case. In our work, we have found that elementary school students from all over the United States have written candid comments about what they have accomplished, how they think they could improve their work, and which activities they did and did not understand. (p. 31)

Even students as young as kindergartners can learn to identify aspects of good work (Sperling, 1993). For example, primary level students can choose their very best handwriting sample and tell why they selected it. They can discuss and compare two writing samples, and they can talk their way through the best way to solve a problem long before they know the algorithms for doing so on paper. As teachers assist young learners in practicing informal methods of self-assessment, they gradually ease them into more formal methods.

For example, the self-evaluation form in Figure 9.1 asks kindergarten students to assess the task of creating a booklet on the concept of families that will be included in their portfolio. The teacher taught the concept of family as people who live together and support one another. Students learned about different kinds of families such as two-parent families, foster families, one-parent families, families with stepparents, guardians, and the like and discussed ways in which family members can support one another. The self-evaluation form was presented to students at the beginning of their work and was read to students prior to the binding of the booklets so that students could make modifications to their work before publishing. The teacher also included a conference with each student to discuss student work in light of the completed evaluation form. This also gave the teacher a chance to assess the oral self-reflective abilities of individual students.

Self-Evaluation Form for Families Booklet

Directions: Listen while your teacher reads the standard aloud. Look carefully at your work on that standard and circle the answer that best tells about your work.

---

1. The booklet has a picture of my family and a sentence telling about how I support my family.

Yes   Not yet

2. The booklet has 3 pictures of 3 other kinds of families. These are families of 3 children in my class.

Yes   Not yet

3. It is easy to tell who each person is in each family because the name of the person is neatly labeled near his or her picture.

Yes   Not yet

4. There is a picture and a sentence about how my family supports one another.

Yes   Not yet

5. Each sentence begins with a capital letter and ends with a period.

Yes   Not yet

6. The booklet has a title page with the title and my name as author and illustrator.

Yes   Not yet

Figure 9.1 Self-evaluation form for families booklet

After the booklet is completed and bound, the teacher can use the same evaluation form for a benchmark sample, adding specific feedback on the quality of work and the students goals for continued improvement.

Older students in the intermediate grades learn the process of self-assessment in much the same way as younger students. In the beginning, it will be difficult for many students to assess themselves because they simply are not used to doing so. The teacher will need to model self-evaluation techniques and demonstrate the use of checklists and rubrics in the beginning, but students will soon internalize and apply these standards to their work (Marzano, Pickering, & McTighe, 1993).

A note on the use of circles with faces in them as choices for younger students to mark their response to self-assessment questions: Such response choices include a happy face smile that presumably indicates satisfaction with one's work, a face with a straight line for a mouth (which could indicate mild satisfaction, not knowing, or a host of other things), and a distinctly sad face with a downturned mouth showing displeasure with one's work. The wise primary level teachers from Diven Elementary School in Elmira, New York, feel that the use of these faces detracts from the focus on an accurate self-assessment because they so heavily focus on an affective judgment. In the eyes of young children, the selection of a happy face every time is almost irresistible as it would not be acceptable for their work to make someone sad-faced. It's an important distinction to consider when the need for belonging in young children is often tied directly to whether their teacher and others like them or not. Therefore the teachers at Diven School recommend the use of short-answer responses that young children can easily understand and that relate directly to the question being asked.

THE METHODS OF SELF-ASSESSMENT

A wide array of self-assessment methods has been reported in the assessment literature—methods that can be used effectively in single-task assessment as well as portfolio assessment. When selecting self-assessment methods, most teachers advise starting wherever one feels comfortable so that the management of reviewing forms and conferring with students does not seem overwhelming. Any or all of the following can be used to effectively assist students in reflecting on their work as they evaluate work quality and prepare to make goals for improvement.

Reflective Journals

These have a variety of names that correspond with their intended purpose (i.e., writer's journal, math journal, literature response journal, learning logs). In any reflective journal, students record observations, feelings, insights, and judgments about their work and themselves as learners. Most teachers hesitate to use journals as open-ended self-assessment until students become proficient at using journals. Instead, teachers use prompts and probes such as the following to help students focus on learning as an ongoing, dynamic process (Taggart, Phifer, Nixon, & Wood, 1998):

- How do I learn best?
- What is still unclear to me?
- What is getting easier?

- What are my strengths?
- Where do I need to improve and how should I go about it?
- How am I functioning in group work?
- How can the teacher help me to improve?

Teachers who use journals find that, if they spend time up front modeling helpful responses, students will write productive entries. Teacher responses to journals should be constructed so that students deepen their answers to questions and continue to think about themselves as learners. Collecting four or five journals a day eases the work of writing responses for teachers and, given a class size of twenty-five, students can benefit from specific teacher feedback approximately every week.

Checklists

Checklists can help students evaluate their progress in developing good work habits and organizational skills, many of which can be found on report cards. For example, listening to others, persistence in tasks, ability to take turns, and ability to work well with others are just a sampling of the kinds of work habits and sense of organization that teachers feel are necessary for the production of quality work. Teachers can take the opportunity to demonstrate what should happen in a collaborative work environment by asking students to help select the items on any checklist that will be used for evaluation purposes. Figures 9.2 and 9.3 are examples of typical checklists used for self-evaluation of work habits and organizational skills.

Editing Checklist

Directions: Read each of the items below. Read your story aloud to a friend. Make an X on the blank if you think the item tells about your story.

1. _____The title goes with the story.

2. _____The beginning is interesting.

3. _____There are many descriptive words that add to the story.

4. _____Each sentence starts with a capital letter and ends with a period (.), a question mark (?), or an exclamation point (!).

5. _____The ending makes sense.

FIGURE **9.2**   Checklist for editing skills

Small-Group Discussion Checklist

Directions: Read each item and think about the role you played in the small-group discussion exercise. Put an X under the answer that best describes your behavior throughout the discussion.

Item	Frequently	Sometimes	Not Yet
I listened to other people's ideas.			
I gave support to ideas I thought were good.			
I contributed useful ideas of my own.			
I modified my thinking when I heard an idea that made sense to me.			
I helped the group move toward our goal.			

Please write down any behaviors that helped you to feel successful in this group exercise. _____

_____

_____

_____

FIGURE 9.3 Group discussion checklist (ability to work well with others)

The argument for using all methods of self-assessment, and checklists in particular, is that students will become self-regulating learners if they have a chance to monitor their own behaviors. Every time students think about an item on a checklist, they move a step forward in empowering themselves.

Peer Interactions

Much is written about peer interactions such as peer evaluation, peer assessment, peer review, peer conferencing, peer tutoring, and peer editing. The commonality among these is that they all involve students sharing work with other students. Most often this is done in pairs selected by the teacher. Also, all peer interactions should be carefully planned, modeled, and monitored by the teacher.

The techniques of peer evaluation and peer assessment deserve closer examination by all teachers and perhaps some cautionary advice is in order when deciding which peer interaction to select. Evaluations, or assessments, are usually done by people who are experts in the task or process at hand. Such expert status is rarely attained by the typical elementary student. In addition, it may not be wise to ask elementary-school-aged peers to judge their friend's work as "good" or "bad". The need for friendship and belonging, which is so strong in elementary students, might taint the accuracy of the evaluation or assessment. Also, peers judging another peer's work does little to foster student self-assessment.

Regardless of the teacher's selection, all kinds of peer interactions need to provide *both* students with a chance to benefit from the interaction. For example, checklists and some rubrics can be useful in providing peers with a chance to practice organizational and editing skills with work other than their own. The peer who receives the feedback can analyze the feedback in order to determine which modifications to make, if any. Also, providing students with focus or clarifying questions to structure the conference increases the chance that self-assessment is taking place and "judgmental telling" is kept to a minimum (see Figure 9.4).

Such questions help to guide the conference to an acceptable conclusion for both students. The peer reviewer is assisted with a productive focus for the conference and the writer gets to talk about his or her work, a powerful self-assessment tool in itself. No matter which methods of self-assessment teachers use, the outcome should be that students are prepared for a goal-setting conference with the teacher.

FEEDBACK CONFERENCES AND GOAL-SETTING

A valuable part of self-assessment is getting quality feedback from others and using it to make modifications in existing work as well as setting goals for future work. Conferences between students and students and between students and the teacher help students to become aware of how others see their work and to get assistance in setting performance enhancing goals. Careful planning of student to student interactions and conferences can yield a productive goal-setting conference time of around twenty minutes. However, making the time for student conferences is the single most-challenging task for elementary teachers. For example, with a class of twenty-five students a teacher will need to find a precious eight hours and twenty minutes in order to have one-on-one conferences with each student. The following lists possible times during the day when teachers can call students for conferences:

Peer Conference Record for Writing

Name_____   Date _____

Directions: Please use these questions to have a conversation about your current piece of writing with your peer.

1. What is the title of the piece you are working on?
2. What kind of writing is it?
3. Tell me something about it.
4. Tell me something about the writing that you're having difficulty with.
5. What, specifically, can I help you with?
6. Tell me what you like best about this piece?

Peer comments:
(Please discuss the strengths of this person's writing work.)

_____

_____

_____

FIGURE **9.4**   Peer conference form for writing

- During the time when students are working independently on learning centers
- During writers' workshop time
- During snack time
- When several students are out of the classroom for "pull out" classes (i.e., band, orchestra, remedial classes, etc.)
- While students are working on a "sponge" activity
- While the entire class is engaging in a peer interaction activity
- After school with students who walk home
- Before school with early arrivals
- During times when teachers "buddy up" their classes and create a read-to-one-another activity

Goal-setting conferences usually take place every six weeks or so in elementary schools. Creative planning and using every available time slot will enable teachers to complete one-on-one conferences in a week and a half.

Teachers of young children who want to complete conferences sooner often schedule volunteers to assist with ongoing instruction so the teacher is free to meet with students.

Once the time is found, what should take place in a goal-setting conference? The outcome of student-teacher conferences should always be the creation of specific short-term goals (i.e., I will learn to use the spell check) and long-term goals (i.e., I will have more patience during group work) by both the student and the teacher. Teacher questioning that asks students to think about their work will assist students in deciding upon goals that will help them to continue to improve. The following prompts can be used to help students prepare for the conference or to elicit useful information during the conference:

- What were the things you liked and disliked about your work on this project?
- What steps did you take to complete this process?
- How and where could you use what you've learned again?
- On which piece of work did you try the hardest, whether you succeeded or not?
- Which piece is your best work? Why?
- Choose any piece of work you think I would choose as your best work. Tell me why.
- What will I learn about you by looking at your portfolio?
- What did you like or dislike about using a portfolio? Why?
- Which piece was most important to your learning? Why?

As the student responds to questions and the teacher is actively listening, the teacher can complete a chart like the one in Figure 9.5.

After the student has verbally listed strengths and goals, the teacher can add additional strengths and goals after a careful review of the work. Both the teacher and the student should retain a copy of this report and it can be used for reporting to parents in addition to checking periodically to see if short- and long-term goals are being met.

Goal-setting opportunities like the ones presented in this chapter are as important to student empowerment as an engine is to a car; such opportunities make student empowerment start and, with continued use, run smoothly. While James Hughes, in the last century before the invention of the motorcar, wouldn't have used the car analogy he would have appreciated the goal and effect of student empowerment. The next section looks at grading authentic tasks and reporting methods that involve parents, students, and teachers.

Results of Goal-Setting Conference

Student Name_____

Date_____

1. The work shows the following student strengths:

2. Goals for continuing improvement are:
   Short-term:

   Long-term:

FIGURE 9.5   Goal-setting conference reporting form

CHAPTER 10

Grading and Reporting Practices

Grades are, unfortunately, an integral part of the American educational system. As early as kindergarten students receive grades that they might not even understand. Ask any teacher what he or she hates most about teaching, and there's a good chance it's "giving grades." Many a teacher has agonized over report cards trying to decide the fate of a student. It is a gut-wrenching task for teachers to translate everything they know about what a student knows, can do, and feels into one single letter or numerical score. That final grade may determine promotion or retention. It may determine placement in a class or school or participation in extracurricular activities. It may determine school honor roll, class ranking, college admission, college scholarship, or career placement. All of these things may be determined by a grading process that rarely guards against teachers being too lenient, rigorous, or arbitrary.

Kay Burke in
How to Assess Authentic Learning

It is report card time and Anthony gives his report card to his parents. He has received three A's, two B's, one C, and a D. Anthony's mother points to the D, which is in mathematics, and asks Anthony why he received this D. Anthony, of course, doesn't know why he received the D nor does he know why he has the A's and B's. Further, Anthony doesn't know what he can do to maintain the "good" grades and has no suggestions for how to improve upon the other grades. Anthony's mother requests a conference with the teacher in order to find out what the teacher perceives to be Anthony's strengths and what he can do in order to improve his work. At the conference, Anthony's mother is presented with Anthony's test scores and homework completion data for the marking period and little else. The conference is merely an exercise in looking at grades and how they were weighted and averaged. Anthony's mother goes home and tells Anthony to try harder.

Unfortunately, this scenario plays itself out far too often. If grades are a method of reporting the level of learning to students and parents, then practices similar to that described above fall far short of the mark. Fortunately, there is a movement away from such teacher-centered grading methods as described above and a movement toward a more student-centered, authentic assessment approach including the use of portfolios. Research on portfolio assessment indicates that portfolios have a positive impact on the insight students have about their own academic strengths and goals for improvement (O'Neill, 1993). The use of portfolio assessment would have provided Anthony with access to the specific evaluation criteria by which his work would be judged and provided him with ample self-assessment and goal-setting opportunities. Given this, the chances are increased that Anthony would be able to have a productive conference with his parents who could assist him in meeting his short- and long-term goals. The focus of this section is to show how authentic assessments can be used to report, in a useful way, to students and parents on the quality of learning that has taken place over a reporting period.

GRADING ISSUES

The advent of giving letter grades and, even worse, percentage grades to student work began with the mass movement to quantify intelligence and learning. Content areas were rigidly divided and reporting systems were established that reduced learning to tasks that were easily quantifiable. Grades, not the learning, became the assessment in the minds of many instead of what grades really are, a technique used to report the outcome of an assessment. Important decisions on retention and promotion were based on grades. Everyone seemed to understand the judgment, "She's a D-plus student," or "He's a B-minus in reading". Almost no one moved backwards from the B-minus to the assessments that led to the grade, nor even further back to the learning that led to the assessments that were used to calculate the grade. Teachers became so confident of these judgments that it was assumed that little explanation need be given to anyone, even students and parents. The implication for teaching was also ignored when acknowledging the B-minus as a significant outcome in itself.

Thankfully, the results of the long-term practice of grading has been carefully studied and much has been learned about the effect of the enormous attention paid to grades by American education. For example, grades oversimplify the complexity of learning, are often arbitrary, foster unhealthy competition and comparisons among students, and are not effective motivators for anyone, especially weak students. John Goodlad (1994) who has extensively studied the practices of teachers and the effect of those practices on students says this of conventional assessment and grading practices:

We are content to use various combinations of the first six letters of the alphabet and two digits representing either total scores or percentile rankings as virtually the sole basis for judging the adequacy of an individual's or a school's performance. . . .

My proposition is that the conventional means of assessing achievement are inadequate criteria of school success and corrupt the educative process. If we are to use student outcomes as a major measure of school and student performance—and I assume we will for a long time to come—then let us at least endeavor to appraise that performance on the basis of those goals for which our schools are responsible. This means developing and using tests related to the content and experiences that have been used to attain these goals. (p. 59)

Speaking of conventional methods of testing in particular, Howard Gardner (1987) advised educators to get away altogether from tests and correlation among tests and look instead at more naturalistic sources of information about how peoples around the world develop skills important to their way of life. Measures of authentic assessment facilitate Gardner's idea by measuring instruction that asks students to probe, think about, and examine learning that evolved from carefully selected content or lifelong standards. At the same time, the importance of grades seems to be firmly entrenched in American schooling and change seems far off on the horizon. The good news is that authentic assessments and grading systems are not mutually exclusive.

GRADING AUTHENTIC ASSESSMENTS

While there is agreement that authentic assessments can be graded, teachers understand that authentic assessment offers much more than can be captured meaningfully in a single grade or set of grades (Seidel & Walters, 1997). The question every good teacher needs to wrestle with, then, is "We know we *can* grade authentic assessments, but *should* we?" As with any good question, there is rarely a simple answer and the answer to this one is, it depends.

Consider, for example, that most schools still use conventional report cards that ask teachers to separate learning into specific content areas and to give students a letter grade or its equivalent to each content area. In such report cards, there normally is not even a hint of what the curricula or instruction were like during the marking period. The sole use of this kind of report card for reporting student progress to students and parents is highly discouraged because it tells very little about the quality of teaching and learning during the marking period. Instead, good elementary teachers are able to surmount this communication problem by sending home supporting evidence (rubrics, checklists, and portfolios) with the report card so that progress is more richly reported. Given that most teachers will need to assign grades or their equivalents to student work, there are several things to consider when deciding which authentic assessments to grade and how to do so.

Holistic Scoring Rubrics

Teachers with little or no experience in using authentic assessments, including portfolios, often believe that judgments based on such assessments are largely opinion, whereas conventional grades reflect consistently applied standards of quality. Barton and Collins (1997) found that the reverse is much more likely to be true:

> On a number of occasions we have asked teachers to individually grade the same piece of student writing. Without fail, teachers assigned grades that ranged from A to D. When asked to justify their decisions, teachers focused on different aspects of the written piece; some teachers were more interested in the conventions of writing, others placed greater value in the expression of ideas, and still others were concerned about coherence. (p. 86)

These kinds of inconsistencies occur less often when holistic scoring rubrics with specific evaluation criteria are used. Holistic scoring is the practice of giving an overall evaluation to a product without analyzing the strengths or weaknesses of each part of the product separately. In a writing assignment, for instance, grammar, punctuation, and spelling would not be graded individually but would be considered in the overall sense of fluency and expression of ideas. Holistic rubrics help build bridges from letter grades to actual instruction and intended learning standards by elaborately and clearly defining exactly what is represented by an A, B, or C. Several teachers, using the same holistic writing rubric, will all have very consistent scoring, or grading, results. Therefore, it is acknowledged that rubrics are a more effective and less teacher-dependent description of student work than a simple letter grade that is based on criteria that are not clearly defined or that are given inordinate weight by the teacher.

In addition to providing teachers with scoring consistency, holistic rubrics, in particular, provide teachers with an opportunity to clarify for students what an A, B, C, or D product or process looks like. It is important to remember that the purpose of a student assessment is to improve performance, not just audit it; assessment should instruct students and faculty alike about what outstanding work is (Wiggins, 1996). For example, the holistic rubric in Figure 10.1 would characterize an A paper as follows:

Holistic Writing Rubric

Criteria	A	B	C	D
Responding to the Task	Stays on the topic very well and writes in an imaginative and interesting way	Stays on the topic very well	Writes about the topic but doesn't stay on the topic	Hardly writes about the topic
Organization	Writing shows good planning. There are bridges between paragraphs and ideas are explained well	Writing shows good planning and ideas are explained well. Paragraphs and sentences are in order	Ideas are out of order and, instead of staying with one idea at a time, there is some jumping around	Sentences are not in order and the ideas are not explained
Details	Uses many details which explain the topic well	Uses enough details to explain the topic	Uses few details to explain the topic	Does not give details to explain the topic, or gives details that do not go with the topic
Sentences	Uses sentence variety in a meaningful and interesting way	Has some sentence variety (different kinds, different length)	Writes in sentences but most of them are alike or start the same way	Does not write in sentences
Vocabulary and Language	Uses descriptive and specific words	Uses words and language that are right for the topic	Uses tired and overused words	Uses immature words
Mechanics	Makes very few grammar, spelling, and punctuation errors	Some grammar, spelling, and punctuation errors but they do not make reading or understanding difficult	Spelling, grammar and punctuation errors make the piece difficult	Many spelling, grammar, and punctuation errors which make it very difficult to understand the assignment

An F is earned if the writing piece is totally off the topic *or* cannot be read *or* cannot be understood.

FIGURE 10.1   Holistic writing rubric by Roberta Senzer and Language Arts Collaborative, Harborfields CSD (NY)

- The paper would be mechanically nearly error-free;
- Planning for writing would be evident through staying on the topic, developing the topic by using supporting details, and having smooth transition between paragraphs; and
- The writing would be interesting, descriptive, and detailed.

Naturally, models of "A papers" would be presented to students as the process of writing is taught and practiced. Grant Wiggins (1996) says that, unless students are constantly exposed to the best possible products, performances, and specifications in each field, they will never produce the best work that they are capable of producing. Examples of B, C, and D papers would also be presented to students after the standards for an A were examined and practiced. The benefit of presenting substandard examples is to provide students with a chance to practice editing and proofreading skills. This focus on standards helps teachers grade student work against the standards and helps stop student to student comparisons.

For each criterion on the rubric, the teacher can use portfolio contents, samples over time, checklists, student self-assessment and any other relevant pieces of student work to determine where the student is for that particular criterion. Holistic scoring rubrics can also be used to assess single pieces of student work and they can be designed for any content task.

Portfolios

Regardless of the specific purpose and contents of a portfolio, many items in the portfolio can be graded if a teachers wishes to do so. Some teachers even feel confident enough with making an overall assessment of the portfolio in the form of a grade. The grade is often related to descriptive criteria such as the following:

A = Exceeds Expectations
B = Meets Expectations
C−D = In Progress of Meeting Expectations
F = Does Not Meet Expectations

Such criteria report in a global fashion, with the individual contents of the portfolio providing the teacher, student, and parent with supporting evidence for the grade. The focus should always be on the learning that has taken place, whether a grade is given or not given. In addition, teachers need to abandon the idea behind conventional methods of grading that call for practices such as averaging scores. For example, it would be poor practice indeed to average all the grades in a portfolio for the purpose of assigning a grade to the entire portfolio. One needs to consider the kinds of descriptors to use, which are represented by the grades, and the weights given to individual tasks and test scores contained in the portfolio. Each piece of assessment data can be factored into the whole assessment picture depending on its value to the whole picture as determined by the teacher. The bottom-line question to be answered by every teacher in deciding what to grade is "To what extent does this report on the learning that has taken place throughout the course of this marking period?" If the answer is "It doesn't", then it probably is not a necessary piece of the assessment picture.

Many teachers are discovering that it is most helpful if the standard-based criteria used in authentic assessments match the criteria used on report cards. Because teachers feel that changing conventional report cards is an essential step in the alignment of curriculum, instruction, and assessment, many are willing to give their time and expertise in designing a report card that is more in alignment with instruction.

STANDARDS-BASED REPORTING SYSTEMS

Some schools or school districts have a report card in place that is reflective of standards and includes evaluation criteria that report on progress toward meeting those standards. For example teachers in the Elmira City School District in Elmira, New York, developed a report card that contains the following sections that include carefully selected, specific evaluation criteria:

- Listening and Speaking
- Social and Work Study Skills
- Literacy (Subdivided into a Reading Rubric and a Writing Rubric)
- Integrated Units of Study including 1) Ongoing Processes, 2) Mathematics, 3) Science/Health, and 4) Social Studies
- Fine Arts and Physical Education

There are two keys for teacher marking:

Marking Key	Effort Key
4. Applies skills & concepts independently	E-Excellent
3. Applies skills & concepts with some assistance	S-Satisfactory
2. Is developing skills & concepts	I-Improving
1. Is experiencing difficulty	
☐ Not applicable at this time	

It is important to note that the descriptors under the marking key clearly indicate that the goal of learning is to go beyond mere knowledge acquisition. For example, the highest expectation or standard is that students are able to independently *apply* skills and concepts in their work. The implication for instruction, then, is that lessons and activities involving higher level thinking are expected to occur so students can practice their application level skills.

Figure 10.2 shows the section on Integrated Units of Study, which reflects student work in a variety of content areas, all of which are integrated into units. This section deserves closer examination in order to see the possibility for marking learning progress in separate content areas that occurred within an integrated instructional approach.

Clearly, such a report card tells a great deal about the learning that took place during the marking period. When this Progress Report is combined with illustrative samples of student work such as the portfolio contents, students, parents, and other teachers are provided with a comprehensive picture of student growth and achievement (O'Malley & Pierce, 1996). Even though grades appear to be an American institution, every attempt to explain how a child is doing in school will make the grade much less important than the learning.

The next chapter presents the benefits of student-led conferences and describes a method for implementing student-parent-teacher conferences with a focus on specific goals for future learning opportunities.

Integrated Units of Study

Dec. _____

March _____

June _____

Ongoing Processes	Dec.	March	June
Explains information orally and/or in writing			
Makes connections between content areas			
Uses one or more strategies to solve a problem			
Uses estimation, inquiry & experimentation to predict and check solutions/results			
Identifies & uses patterns			
Uses available technologies to design, construct & evaluate products			
Mathematics			
Mathematical Reasoning			
Number and Numeration			
Operations			
Modeling/Multiple Representation			
Measurement			
Uncertainty (Estimation & Probability)			
Patterns/Functions			
Science/Health			
Earth Sciences			
Life Sciences			
Physical Sciences			
Social Studies			
US & NYS History			
World History			
Geography			
Economics			
Civics/Citizenship/Government			

FIGURE 10.2   Sample section of elementary progress report from the Elmira City School District, Elmira, NY

CHAPTER **11**

Student-Led Conferences

I would like to leave a parent-teacher conference with a solid idea of how my son is doing in school. I would like to see work in every area that Mike did and have the teacher's honest appraisal of his work. I want Mike there too so he can talk about his reactions to his work and the lessons he is getting. I want to know what kind of a worker he is and how I can help him at home. I want a chance to discuss some problem areas I see and have the teacher spend time to work on solutions with me. Mike is in the fourth grade now and, since kindergarten, I've been told he's a B student and that he talks too much in class. This is what I take off work for. We never seem to get anywhere.

Sonja Kim,
mother of Michael Kim

Parent involvement in schools is a hot topic in education today. Teachers are often heard to say that parents "don't care". Even in schools with high parent conference attendance, teachers complain that the "right" parents aren't there, meaning the parents of the children who are the least successful. Parents say that schools make them feel intimidated or powerless and that school actions often serve to alienate parents. These parents report incidences where they were asked to take off work in order to attend a fifteen-minute obligatory "conference" (children not invited) which consisted of going over the grades on a report card. Other parents, who get a longer conference, often get the impression that the teacher does not want or value input from the parents because the focus of the conference is clearly on what the teacher thinks about the student's work.

Parents feel both cheated and frustrated by such conferencing behaviors. While these practices are disappearing, many teachers and parents alike confess that conference times are unproductive and fruitless. Both blame the problems of society on what is often viewed by many citizens as an intractable problem of communication between the home and school. This view is very evident in newspapers across America that are filled with letters to the editor about teachers not doing their jobs and parents who do not have time in their busy lives to monitor the work and behaviors of their children. Such generalizations are damaging to everyone. The truth of the matter is that something needs to be changed to reflect what parents and teachers really are like. Parents care about their children, teachers care about their students, and all stakeholders in the school system need to work together to ensure that parent involvement is a meaningful, rewarding, and integral part of a child's schooling.

The following cautions and considerations (Shalaway, 1993) should be kept in mind by all school personnel when rethinking how to enhance parent involvement:

- Realize that teacher evaluations of their children affect many parents' own sense of self-worth.
- Be flexible with conference times to accommodate parent's work schedules.
- Recognize the changes in family structure in today's world. Invite divorced or separated parents to meet with teachers individually, if they prefer to do so.

The long history of fruitless, unproductive, even negative effects of conventional parent conferences should be recognized by teachers and principals. This chapter describes a method that can help to establish positive and meaningful parent involvement.

STUDENTS AT THE CENTER OF THE PROCESS

As has been discussed throughout this book, methods of authentic assessment are student-centered. Students are actively engaged in authentic tasks, they receive and use feedback from teachers, peers, and parents, and they set goals for their continued improvement. With the goal of creating self-regulated learners, students are clearly at the center of the learning process.

Both teachers and parents impact greatly on student learning, with teachers seeming to have the most influence on learning after a child begins school. This does not mean, however, that parental influence is over or even that it should be over. Wise teachers know that the student will benefit from continual parent involvement and want cooperation and help from parents. A good way to begin to establish cooperation is to understand that frequent, informal contact and warm, respectful, honest communication are essential ingredients of effective cooperation (Herrera & Wooden, 1988).

Authentic assessment methods can help parents and teachers become partners who impact upon and focus on the learning of the student. For example, every time a unit of study begins, good teachers send a letter home that explains the nature of the unit and describes some of the authentic tasks that students will be expected to complete. This is a necessary step in building cooperation between home and school because *parents cannot possibly monitor their child's learning unless they know what is going on in advance of the learning.* Some teachers say that sending home information on curriculum and instruction is far too time consuming. Other teachers say that informing parents about upcoming units can increase the chance that parents will help, if they can. Ways in which parents can help are by reinforcing skills at home, finding guest speakers, and making games and other learning materials, to name a few possibilities. In addition, parents may have some time or materials to donate to the unit to be studied and the whole class may benefit from this extra help. The point here is that we can be sure that parents will *not* be involved in their child's work if no one tells them what is happening in school *before* it happens. Newsletters explaining last month's grade-level accomplishments after the fact just don't serve to involve parents in the learning process in a significant way. At the same time, when parents receive a newsletter from the teacher, it would be a link in the chain of cooperation to send the teacher a complimentary note on something with which parents were impressed.

Given that students are at the center of the learning process and that parent involvement is highly desirable, the following illustrates possible steps that could be taken in a classroom that uses methods of authentic assessment and that has student empowerment as a major goal. The steps provide an overview of how a student-centered conference time could evolve.

- In advance of teaching an integrated unit of study, the teacher sends a letter to parents that describes the tasks and methods of assessment that will be included in the upcoming unit work. (See sample letter in Figure 11.1.)
- The teacher appropriately incorporates suggestions and assistance from parents into the unit plan. The teacher and students proceed through the unit work that includes completion of a portfolio and student self-assessment.
- Parent feedback is solicited concerning parent impressions about how and what their child is learning. (See sample form in Figure 11.2.)
- The students plan a "Portfolio Party" upon completion of the unit work and invite parents and significant others. (See invitation in Figure 11.3.)
- Students, teachers, and parents prepare for a conference:

- The teacher uses authentic assessments and conventional assessments to complete the report card (one, hopefully, that is in alignment with curriculum and instruction).
- The student reviews the report card and establishes goals for short-term and long-term needs. (See Figure 11.4.)
- The student has a student-parent conference at home using the report card and completed goal-setting form.
- Parents assist the student with any additional goals and offer ways to help the student to meet those goals.
- The student-led conference with parents, the student, and the teacher is held.

The work that is completed leading up to the conference is all effort that will empower students to become self-regulated learners. The outcome of the conference should be an appropriate and clear list of short- and long-term goals and specific ways in which those goals will be met.

A DEPICTION OF THE CONFERENCE METHOD

Kristy Ruwet, a fourth-grade teacher, planned a unit on Seeds and Plants for her students. As she planned authentic learning tasks, she also planned the methods of assessment she would use so she could clearly communicate to students her expectations for quality work. A large part of the unit assessment included the making of a portfolio and Ms. Ruwet also planned a portfolio party so students could "publish" their work. The work in this unit would be included in the progress report and the goal-setting conference.

In advance of teaching the unit, Ms. Ruwet sent the following letter home to parents:

Dear Parents,
    We will soon begin work on a unit called *The World of Seeds and Plants*. This unit will contain a variety of engaging activities and sources of information to aid all types of learners. It will integrate the content areas of science, math, language arts, and social studies. Active learning activities that mirror what people do in real life are planned. These include:

- planting seeds and keeping a daily journal of growth
- experimenting with variables that affect plant growth
- creating a map of the United States using clay
- researching state flowers and locating the state on their map

- dissecting fruits, plants, and seeds
- simulating the pollination process
- writing letters and stories
- sorting, counting, and graphing seeds and their growth
- tracing the life cycle of a seed

An important learning strategy that helps students to understand and remember information well is guided discovery. Some concepts surrounding plants and seeds that students will discover through the work in this unit are:

- the life cycle of seeds
- the importance of plants to peoples' lives
- how animals affect plants

An essential part of this unit is the use of the problem-solving model. Students will apply this model in several activities as they discover new things about seeds and plants.

Throughout the unit, students will be asked to self-assess the quality of their work. This helps students to take responsibility for their learning and gives them an opportunity to reflect on their work and make any necessary modifications. Students will compile a portfolio of their work and "publish" their work at a Portfolio Party to which you will be invited.

Because the entire class welcomes parent involvement, please complete the following two questions and return your responses to school via your child.

Thank you for your continuing support,

Ms. Kristy Ruwet

1. Is there something you would like me to plan for in this unit on Seeds and Plants? If so, please describe below.
2. Is there something you can contribute to this unit? Please elaborate and include your phone number so that I may call you.

FIGURE 11.1   Sample letter to parents

As Ms. Ruwet collects the parent responses, she discovers that parent ideas include wanting the children to make a terrarium and wanting them to visit a local greenhouse. In addition, some parents volunteered to send in seeds and plants. Ms. Ruwet decides to incorporate these things into the unit on seeds and plants and arranges for students to write thank-you notes to the parent helpers.

Midway through the unit, Ms. Ruwet sends a parent feedback form home in order to encourage a parent-student dialogue about how and what the child is learning as a result of unit work (see Figure 11.2).

Parent Feedback Form

The World of Seeds and Plants

Dear Parents,

In preparation for the upcoming conferences, I would like you to talk with your child about his or her work on the current unit *The World of Seeds and Plants*. This information will help your child, you, and me to establish goals and specific ways to meet those goals by the time of the conference. Please write your responses to the questions and send this paper to school with your child.

1. What does your child like best about this unit?
2. What does your child like least about this unit?
3. What is your child excited about in this unit?
4. What is your child having difficulty with in this unit?
5. What suggestions do you have to smooth out these difficulties?
6. What questions do you have about this unit?

Thank you very much for your valuable help. We hope you will be able to come to our Portfolio Party during the evening of March 7th.

Sincerely,

Ms. Ruwet

FIGURE **11.2**   Parent feedback form

As students bring completed feedback forms to school, the teacher uses the opportunity to have a miniconference with each child. For children who do not return a form, Ms. Ruwet has a longer conference so that these children get to respond to all questions on the form did as those children who completed the process with their parents.

Students continue to complete unit work and soon it is time for the Portfolio Party (see Figure 11.3 for a sample invitation). At the party, students will present their portfolios to someone and answer questions about their work. Students are encouraged to invite anyone whom they think will be able to come and the teacher will make sure that every child has someone with whom to share their work.

Of course, if a teacher determines that the chance of getting almost all parents to come to school for the party is not very good, then other avenues for audiences need to be explored. Students could invite another class or a

Portfolio Party Invitation

*You
are cordially invited
to our*

*Portfolio
Party*

Where: Ms. Ruwet's Classroom
When: Tuesday, March 7th, 7:00 to 8:00

Our portfolios on *The World of Seeds and Plants*
will be on display and there will be
things to eat and drink.

FIGURE 11.3   Sample portfolio party invitation

group of adults in the school (i.e., principal, school nurse, counselor, lunch aide, other teachers, or janitor) and have the party during the school day. Regardless of who the audience is, the students get a chance to share and talk about their work, an important contributor to accurate self-assessment.

In preparation for the upcoming home-school conference, the student receives the report card completed by the teacher and has a conference with parents about their work during the marking period. Ms. Ruwet has included a goal-setting form for the student and parents to complete prior to the conference (see Figure 11.4). This at-home conference helps the student and parents focus on strengths to date and specific goals for improvement.

The at-school parent/teacher/student conference is scheduled and the student leads the discussion by referring to strengths shown during the marking period and by giving evidence for those strengths. Parents and the teacher can ask questions and help the child with setting realistic goals and ways to meet those goals.

Both the teacher and the parents can encourage the student to add strengths and goal as they see fit and the student can cite examples from completed work to give evidence for their judgments. The student is assisted

Goal-Setting Form

Name Marvin Edmonds

Marking Period March 8th–April 16th

Date of Conference with Parents April 17, 2000

The following are strengths I have shown in this marking period:

I have done all my work to the best of my ability.

My handwriting looks better because I am holding my pencil right.

I raise my hand when I want to talk and I get most of the answers right.

My written work is better when I read it out loud because I am taking my time with my writing and not hurrying to get it done.

I read 18 books and had 15 reader's conferences.

I wrote 5 stories on the computer.

I work without disturbing others most of the time.

I have the following goals for improvement for my work in the next marking period:

1. I need to do more math problems at home for practice so I don't forget how to do them the next day.

2. I will listen more during group work and stop fooling around.

3. My spelling needs to be better.

I will do the following to help me meet my goals.

1. I will bring my math papers home and ask someone to give me some problems to do just like the ones I did in school.

2. I will ask other kids to give me a signal in group work when I need to stop fooling around.

3. I will keep a spelling log of all the words I need to spell right.

Halfway through the next marking period, I will meet with my parents at home and we will talk about how well I am meeting my goals. I will report to my teacher what we talked about at the conference.

Marvin Edmonds
Student Signature

FIGURE 11.4   Sample completed goal-setting form

with any means to reach the agreed-upon goals and everyone consents to monitoring the progress made throughout the next marking period.

Such examples of student-led conferences on work completed in a collaborative learning environment help students to take responsibility for their learning. Student responsibility is what both teachers and parents want and behaving responsibly toward learning heads the student in the right direction toward becoming a productive citizen and a lifelong learner. Student led conferences can have this outcome if authentic learning tasks and authentic assessment are planned, complete with specific evaluation criteria and student self-assessment. Authentic assessment is the means to the outcome of quality instruction and students being empowered to learn.

Perhaps Mrs. Kim's comments would look like this, after a parent-teacher conference led by her son Michael:

> I could not believe how serious Mike was about evaluating his own learning. Before the conference, he made sure I understood exactly what he had studied and what his work looked like. I was truly amazed and proud of his portfolio. We went through it page by page and Mike told me exactly what he was good at and what he needed to do better. He asked me if he could read his work out loud to me sometimes because that helped him to catch his mistakes. By the time we got to the parent-teacher conference, I felt like most of it was already done. The three of us talked about what changes to make for the next report period.

This is the kind of engagement that all stakeholders can achieve when authentic assessments are used. Teachers teach with more confidence because of the alignment of standards, curriculum, instruction, and assessment. Students work hard to meet standards because the students are recognized as integral parts of the process of teaching and learning. They experience relevancy and clarity in completing authentic tasks and assessments and students are empowered by self-assessment and goal-setting opportunities. Parents have a better understanding of what their child is doing in school as well as how they are doing. The effect of using authentic assessment is best summed up in the words of Elbert Hubbard:

> The object of teaching children is to enable them to get along without their teacher.

References

Airasian, P. (1994). *Classroom Assessment.* New York, NY: McGraw-Hill.

Andrade, H. (1997). Understanding rubrics. *Educational Leadership, 54,* 4–8.

Armstrong, T. (1995). *Multiple intelligences in the classroom.* Alexandria, VA: Association of Supervision and Curriculum Development.

Azwell, T., & Schmar, E. (1995). *Report card on report cards.* Portsmouth, NH: Heinemann.

Baker, E. (Ed.). (1996). Creating better student assessments. *Improving America's schools: A newsletter on issues in school reform.* Washington: US Department of Education. Available at: <http://www.middleweb.com>

Barton, J., & Collins, A. (Eds.) (1997). *Portfolio assessment: A handbook for educators.* New York: Addison-Wesley.

Belanoff, P., & Dickson, M. (1991). *Portfolios: Process and product.* Portsmouth, NH: Heinemann.

Bond, L., Roeber, E., & Connealy, S. (1998). *Trends in state student assessment programs.* Washington, DC: Council of Chief State School Officers.

Bowers, B. (1989). *Alternatives to standardized educational assessment.* Eugene, OR: ERIC Clearinghouse on Educational Management (ERIC Document Reproduction Service No. ED 312 773).

Bracey, G. (1993). Assessing the new assessments. *Principal, 72,* 34–36.

Brooks, J., & Brooks, M. (1993). *In search of understanding: The case for constructivist classrooms.* Alexandria, VA: Association for Supervision and Curriculum Development.

Bruner, J. (1966). *Toward a theory of instruction.* Cambridge, MA: Harvard University Press.

Darling-Hammond, L. (1994). Setting standards for students: The case for authentic assessment. *The Educational Forum. 59,* 14–20.

Darling-Hammond, L., Ancess, J., & Falk, B. (1995). *Authentic assessment in action: Studies of schools and students at work.* New York: Teachers College Press.

Darling-Hammond, L., & Wise, A. (1985). Beyond standardization: State standards and school improvement. *The Elementary School Journal, 85* (3), 315–336.

Dart, B., & Clarke, J. (1991). Helping students become better learners: A case study in teacher education. *Higher Education, 22* (3), 317–35.

Dewey, J. (1916). *Democracy and education.* New York: Free Press.

Dietel, R., Herman, J., & Knuth, R. (1991). *What does research say about assessment?* NCREL, Oak Brook. Available: <http://www.ncrel.org/sdrs/areas/stw_esys/4.assess.htm>

Early elementary resource guide to integrated learning. (1997). Compiled by the University of the State of New York. Albany, NY: New York State Education Department.

Ebenezer, J. & Connor, S. (1998). *Learning to teacher science: A model for the 21st century.* Upper Saddle River, NJ: Merrill.

Eby, J. (1997). *Reflective planning, teaching, and evaluation for the elementary school.* Upper Saddle River, NJ: Prentice-Hall.

Eison, J., Janzow, F., & Pollio, H. (1993). Assessing faculty orientations towards grades and learning: Some initial results. *Psychological Reports, 73* (2), 643.

Ekstrom, R., & Villegas, A. (1994). *College grades: An exploratory study of policies and practices.* New York: College Board Publications.

English Language Arts Standards, (1998). *English language arts: Student performance expectations.* Golden, CO: Instructional Services, Jefferson County Public Schools. Available: <http://204.98.1.2/isu/langarts/intrope.html>

Farr, C. (1991). Cognitive psychology and testing. In K. Green (Ed.), *Educational testing: Issues and applications.* New York: Garland Publishing.

Fazey, D. (1993). Self-assessment as a generic skill for enterprising students: The learning process. *Assessment and Evaluation in Higher Education, 18* (3), 235-50.

Flavell, J. (1979). Metacognition and cognitive monitoring: A new area of cognitive development inquiry. *American Psychologist, 34* (2), 906-11.

Flavell, J. (1985). *Cognitive development (2nd ed.).* Englewood Cliffs, NJ: Prentice-Hall.

Flower, L. (1986). Taking thought: The role of conscious processing in the making of meaning. In E. Maimon, et al. (Eds.), *Thinking, reasoning, and writing.* New York: Longman.

Fuchs, L., Fuchs, D., Hamlet, C. & Ferguson, C. (1992). Within curriculum-based measurement: Using a reading maze task. *Journal of Exceptional Children.* 436-449.

Gagne, E., Yekovich, C., & Yekovich, F. (1993). *The Cognitive Psychology of School Learning.* NY: HarperCollins.

Gardner, H. (1987). Beyond IQ: Education and human development. *Harvard Educational Review, 57* (2), 187-193.

Goodlad, J. (1994). *What schools are for.* Bloomington, IN: Phi Delta Kappa Educational Foundation.

Goulden, N., & Griffin, C. (1995). The meaning of grades based on faculty and student metaphors. *Communication Education, 44* (2), 110-25.

Grabe, M., & Grabe, C. (1998). *Integrating technology for meaningful learning.* New York: Houghton Mifflin.

Grady, J. (1994). *Authentic assessment and tasks: Helping students demonstrate their ability.* National Association for Secondary School Principals (NASSP), *78,* 92-98.

Guthrie, J., & Wigfield, A. (1997). Reading engagement: A rationale for theory and teaching. In J. Guthrie & A. Wigfield (Eds.), *Reading engagement: Motivating reading through integrated instruction.* Newark, DE: International Reading Association.

Hakel, M. (1998). *Beyond multiple choice: Evaluating alternatives to traditional testing for selection.* Mahway, NJ: Lawrence Erlbaum Associates.

Haney, W., & Madaus, G. (1986). *Effects of standardized testing and the future of the National Assessment of Educational Progress.* Working paper for the NAEP study group, Chestnut Hill, MA: Center for the Study of Testing, Evaluation and Educational Policy.

Hart, D. (1994). *Authentic assessment: A handbook for educators.* New York: Addison-Wesley.

Haury, D.L. (1993). Assessing student performance in science. *ERIC CSMEE Digest.* Columbus, OH: ERIC Clearinghouse for Science, Mathematics, and Environmental Education. (ERIC Document Reproduction Service No. ED 359 068).

Haury, D., & Rillero, P. (1994). *Perspectives of hands-on science teaching.* Columbus, OH: The ERIC Clearinghouse for Science, Mathematics, and Environmental Education.

Hein, G., & Price, S. (1994). *Active assessment for active science.* Portsmouth, NH: Heinemann.

Herrera, J., & Wooden, S. (1988). Some thoughts about effective parent-school communication. *Young Children, 17* (4), 78–80.

Hughes, J. (1893). *Mistakes in teaching.* New York: E.L. Kellogg & Company.

Johnson, J., Collins, H., Dupuis, V., & Johansen, J. (1991). *Introduction to the foundations of American education.* Boston: Allyn and Bacon.

Jones, D. (1993). Using authentic assessment in elementary social studies. *Social Science Record, 30,* 17–24.

Kendall, J., & Marzano, R. (1996). *Content knowledge: A compendium of standards and benchmarks for K12 educators.* Aurora, CO: Mid-continent Regional Educational Laboratory.

Kerka, S. (1995). *Techniques for authentic assessments: Practice application brief.* Washington: Office of Educational Research and Improvement.

Kohn, A. (1996). What to look for in a classroom. *Educational Leadership, 54,* 54–55.

Koretz, D. (1983). Arriving in Lake Wobegon: Are standardized tests exaggerating achievement and distorting instruction? *American Educator 12* (2): 8–15, 46–52.

Koretz, D. (1994). *The evolution of a portfolio program: The impact and quality of the Vermont portfolio program in its second Year (1992-93).* Los Angeles, CA: National center for Research on Evaluation, Standards, and Student Testing. (ERIC Document Reproduction Service No. ED 370 983).

Ladd, P., & Hatton, S. (1997). *One district's approach to improving student writing: A study of fourth grade 1991-92 and 1994-95 Kentucky writing portfolios.* Baltimore, MD: Paper presented at the 1997 Annual Conference of the Association for Supervision and Curriculum Development. (ERIC Document Reproduction Service No. ED 409 570).

Liftig, I., Liftig, B., & Eaker, B. (1992). Making assessment work: What teachers should know before they try it. *Science Scope, 15,* 4–6.

Martin-Kniep, G. (1997). Implementing authentic assessment in the classroom, school, and school district. In R. Wiener & J. Cohen (Eds.), *Literacy portfolios: Using assessment to guide instruction.* Upper Saddle River, NJ: Prentice-Hall.

Marzano, R., Pickering, D., & McTighe, J. (1993). *Assessing student outcomes.* Alexandria, VA: Association of Supervision and Curriculum Development.

McColskey, W., & O'Sullivan, R. (1993). *How to assess student performance in science: Going beyond multiple-choice tests.* Tallahassee, FL: Southeastern Regional Vision for Education (SERVE). (ERIC Document Reproduction Service No. ED 363 622).

McLoughlin, J., & Lewis, R. (1998). *Assessing special students.* Upper Saddle River, NJ: Merrill.

Mills-Courts, K., & Amiran, M. (1994). Metacognition and the use of portfolios. In *Portfolios: Process and Product.* P. Belanoff & M. Dickson (Eds.), Portsmouth, NH: Heinemann.

Montgomery County Public Schools, (1997). Just imported from London. *Performance-based assessment task, social studies, grade 5.* Available: <www.mcps.k12.md.us/curriculum/socialstd/MSPAP/>

National Commission on Excellence in Education. (1983). *A nation at risk: The imperative for educational reform.* Washington: US Department of Education.

National Council of Teachers of English (NCTE). (1996). *Standards for the English Language Arts.* Urbana, IL: National Council of Teachers of English.

National Council of Teachers of Mathematics (NCTM). (1998). *Principles and standards for school mathematics: Discussion draft.* Prepared by the Standards 2000 Writing Group. Reston, VA: National Council of Teachers of Mathematics.

National Research Council. (1996). *National science education standards.* Washington: National Academy Press.

National Science Board. (1991). *Science & engineering indicators–1991.* Washington: US Government Printing Office. (NSB 91–1).

New York State Education Department. (1995). *Framework for Social Studies.* Albany, NY: New York State Education Department.

New York state testing program for elementary and intermediate grades: Information brochure. (1997). Monterey, CA: CTB McGraw-Hill.

Nickell, P. (1993). *Alternative assessment: Implications for social studies.* Bloomington, IN: ERIC Clearinghouse for Social Studies/Social Science Education. (ERIC Document Reproduction Service No. ED 360 219.

O'Malley, J., & Pierce, L. (1996). *Authentic assessment for English language learners: Practical approaches for teachers.* New York: Addison-Wesley.

O'Neill, T. (1993). The promise of portfolios. *ASCD Update, 35* (7), 1–5.

Piaget, J. (1973). *To understand is to invent.* New York: Grossman.

Piccolo, J., & Younghans, C. (1994). *Teacher to teacher: A professional's handbook.* Lexington MA: D.C. Health & Company.

Placier, M. (1995). "But I have to have an A": Probing the cultural meanings and ethical dilemmas of grades in teacher education. *Teacher Education Quarterly, 22* (3), 45–63.

Popham, W. (1993). Circumventing the high costs of authentic assessment. *Phi Delta Kappan, 76* (6), 470-473.

Reed, L. (1993). Achieving the aims and purposes of schooling through authentic assessment. *Middle School Journal, 25,* 11-13.

Resnick, L. (1987). *Education and Learning to Think.* Washington: National Academy Press.

Riley, H., et al. (1994). *Current trends in grades and grading practices in undergraduate higher education: Results of the 1992 AACRAO survey.* Washington: American Association of Collegiate Registrars and Admissions Officers.

Rothman, R. (1995). *Measuring up: Standards, assessment, and school reform.* San Francisco: Jossey-Bass Publishers.

Rudner, L. (1993). *Issues and concerns.* [On-line]. Available: Gopher <gopher.ed.gov/Educational Resources, Improvement and Statistics (OREI & NCES)/Educational Resources Information Center (ERIC)/ERIC> Clearinghouse on Assessment and Evaluation/Essays, Bibliographies, & Resources/Alternative Assessment/Issues and Concerns.

Salend, S. (1998). Using portfolios to assess student performance. *Teaching exceptional children, 31, 36-43.*

Schneider, D., et al. (1994). *Expectations of excellence: Curriculum standards for social studies.* Washington: National Council for the Social Studies.

Searfoss, L., Gelfer, J., & Bean, T. (1997). *Developing literacy naturally.* Dubuque, IA: Kendall Hunt.

Seidel, S., & Walters, J. (1997). *Portfolio practices: Thinking through the assessment of children's work.* Washington: National Education Association.

Shalaway, L. (1993). Perfecting parent conferences. *Instructor, 18* (2), 58-65.

Spandel, V. (1994). Making assessment meaningful. *ASCD Update, 36* (6), 1-3.

Sperling, D. (1993). What's worth an 'A'?: Setting standards together. *Educational Leadership, 50* (5), 73-75.

Sternberg, R. (1986). *Intelligence applied: Understanding and increasing your intellectual skills.* San Diego, CA: Harcourt Brace Jovanovich.

Taggart, G., Phifer, S., Nixon, J., & Wood, M. (1998). *Rubrics: A handbook for construction and use.* Lancaster, PA: Technomic Publishing Company.

Thorndike, E. (1913). *Psychology of learning: Educational psychology* (Vol.2). New York: Teachers College Press.

Tierney, R., Carter, M., & Desai, L. (1991). *Portfolio assessment in the reading-writing classroom.* Norwood, MA: Christopher-Gordon Publishers.

Wiener, R., & Cohen, J. (1997). *Literacy portfolios: Using assessment to guide instruction.* Upper Saddle River, NJ: Merrill.

Wiggins, G. (1989). A true test: Toward more authentic and equitable assessment. *Phi Delta Kappan, 49* (8), 35-37.

Wiggins, G. (1990). *The case for authentic assessment.* Washington, DC: ERIC Clearinghouse on Tests, Measurement, and Evaluation. (ERIC Document Reproduction Service No. ED 328 611.)

Wiggins, G. (1996). Anchoring assessment with exemplars: Why students and teachers need models. *The Gifted Child Quarterly, 40* (2), 66-69.

Wildemuth, B. (1984). *Alternatives to standardized tests.* Princeton, NJ: ERIC Clearinghouse on Tests, Measurement, and Evaluation (ERIC Document Reproduction Service No. ED 286 938).

Williams, E. (1992). Student attitudes towards approaches to learning and assessment. *Assessment and Evaluation in Higher Education, 17* (1), 45–58.

Wood, K. (1997). *Interdisciplinary instruction: A practical guide for elementary and middle school teachers.* Upper Saddle River, NJ: Merrill.

Worthen, B. (1993). Critical issues that will determine the future of alternative assessment. *Phi Delta Kappan, 74,* (6), 450–454.

Index

NOTE: Bold page numbers indicate figures